FAMILY PATTERNS

Sheepy Magna.

Burials 1791

William Markham a Pauper Feb:ry ye 25th
William Price April ye 9th
Robert Withnell April ye 12th
Elizabeth Parker a Pauper May ye 29th
Robert Fell Aug:t ye 18th
Mary Alam Dec:r ye 20th

Marriages 1791

Richard Thompson Batchelor of this Parish and Mary Wrash of the same by
    Licence the 3rd of April.

William Bloor of the Parish of Clesbrooke in the County of Leicester Batchelor and
Mary Bradford of this Parish Spinster by Licence the 23rd of June.

Rowland Farmer Okeover of Oldbury in the Parish of Mancester and
Judith Holden of Sheepy Magna by Licence the 30th of June

James Ridley of this Parish Batchelor and Jane Fairfield of the same
    spinster by Licence the 11th of July

Thomas Starkey of this Parish Batchelor and Mary Gilliver of the same
    Spinster by Banns the 20th of October

Edward Rosbottom of this Parish Batchelor and Elizabeth Cooke of Newhouse
in the Parish of Merevale in the County of Warwick Spinster by Licence December ye 24th

Baptisms 1791.

Thomas Son of James Emery and Ann his Wife Jan:ry 9th
Samuel Son of Samuel Wilcocks and Mary his Wife Jan:ry 16th
Charles Son of Thomas Smith and Elizabeth his Wife Jan:ry 26th
William Son of George Hanford and Elizabeth his Wife Jan:ry 30th
Luke Son of Godfrey Fletcher and Sarah his Wife Jan:ry 30th
Sarah Daughter of Charles Starkey and Mary his Wife Mar:h 20th
Thomas Robert Son of Joseph Withnell and Ann his Wife Apr:l 6th
Thomas Son of Thomas Wilson and Sarah his Wife Apr:l 10th
John Son of Thomas Fisher and Joyce his Wife Apr:l 13th
Mary Daughter of John Evans and Sarah his Wife Apr:l 25th
Robert Son of Abraham Marler and Mary his Wife Apr:l 25th
William Son of John Clarke and Susannah his Wife Apr:l 25th

Thomas Brathwaite Curate

Frontispiece: *A Bishop's Transcript of 1791 for Sheepy Parish.*

Family Patterns

A Personal Experience
of Genealogy

by

John Patrick Abbott

KAYE & WARD
LONDON

First published by
Kaye & Ward Ltd
194–200 Bishopsgate
London EC2M 4PA
1971

ISBN 0 7182 0880 3

All enquiries and requests relevant to this title should
be sent to the publisher at the above address and
not to the printer.

Printed in Great Britain by
Richard Clay (The Chaucer Press) Ltd
Bungay, Suffolk

To Catherine and Michael—
the next generation

Contents

Preface

An eighteenth-century clergyman dies old and penniless in the servants' garret of a Leicestershire rectory. A young girl in Birmingham stares horror-struck at a crude drawing of seven coffins. A crusader in the dusty heat of Palestine saves Richard Cœur-de-Lion from captivity by pretending to be the King.

These people, a gulf of years separating them, have only one thing in common, which they never knew. Long after they were dead and all but forgotten, a remote descendant of all three discovered for himself these and many other stories about his ancestors.

This explains the fascination of genealogy, the study of one's ancestors, which until recently was the prerogative of the rich and the powerful. Nowadays, we seem to have at last realized that everyone, however humble, has a family tree; it is a necessary condition of existence and almost everybody is descended from someone of interest or fame. After all, each person has two parents, so that the number of ancestors doubles for each generation one steps back. Eventually, or more logically, primarily, the number of one's ancestors equals the entire population, so that at that stage everyone is descended from everyone else and we are all cousins. This, of course, even when due allowance is made for intermarriage and inbreeding, is very democratic and satisfactory. Thus all Englishmen are descended from Alfred the Great or Wat Tyler, as fancy or sentiment dictate.

Nevertheless, it is much more satisfactory to be able to prove descent, however devious, and it is this search, invariably protracted and frequently disappointing, which occupies the leisure of an increasing number of people today.

It is true that most genealogy is traced only through the male line; following the surname, in fact. This, however, is not always adhered to and many famous pedigrees, of necessity, go through the female line. After all, how else can anyone be descended from famous women of the past? Indeed, even the most eminent family trees frequently have women as links. The Churchill family of the present day is rightly proud of its descent from the first Duke of Marlborough, John Churchill, but it is often forgotten that the Duke's only son died childless and it was a daughter's descendants who assumed the surname again later. The Percy family, of Northumberland, has an illustrious line stretching back for nearly a thousand years, but twice the name has been preserved only by a son-in-law's agreeing to take his wife's name, directly contrary to the normal practice. Oddly enough, the custom of a wife's taking her husband's name on marriage is dictated by tradition and not by law.

Another famous person who bore a name inherited through a female forebear was Oliver Cromwell. Had his great-grandfather not adopted the name of an illustrious uncle, the Lord Protector would have been known to posterity as Oliver Williams; a sad falling off.

Other pedigrees are traced through the female line, with the surname changing. The Queen of England is descended from King Aethelwulf of Wessex and every step can be shown and proved. All the same, the line of royal descent passes through half a dozen women on its way, with consequent changes of surname and dynasty.

With such a distinguished example, who would dare criticize humbler folk for seeking eminent ancestors on the distaff side? After all, plain John Smith's fifth great-grandfather may have married the daughter of a renowned politician or national hero, from whom he is therefore entitled to claim descent. No one can say until the matter has been investigated.

The possibility of such a discovery is one of the reasons why more and more people are turning to genealogy as an absorbing and fascinating hobby. There are other reasons, too. What better way is there of learning about the past, particularly of the social conditions in which people lived, than by studying it through the lives and doings of one's own forebears? This applies particularly today, when the world is changing faster than ever before and the lives of even our grandparents are radically different from our own.

There is, however, yet another incentive to genealogists,

particularly amateurs, and one which is often forgotten. That is the thrill and fascination of research and detection; the excitement of the hunt and the satisfaction when one eventually finds an answer after months, or maybe only minutes, of searching. Crossword puzzles and similar intellectual problems attract many competitors in all kinds of journals but their possibilities pall beside the ramifications and mysteries which baffle and delight the genealogist.

Some years ago I became interested in genealogy and the fascination increased with experience. Although my own family's knowledge of its descent was almost non-existent, there were several stories which had been handed down for two or three generations and even a fragmentary document, with large pieces torn out, which purported to be my paternal grandmother's family tree. It was to the stories that I turned first, however, although they were of varying interest and credibility. I was after no bare list of names and dates, for I wanted to know more about the lives, however humble and uneventful, of those people to whose existence I owed my own. In the event, I was lucky beyond anything I could have hoped for when I started on my quest.

These pages contain the results of several years' research conducted in libraries, churches, record offices and many other places throughout England. In all this I learned my trade as I went along. Genealogy is an amateur's occupation, to be pursued when and how the opportunity permits, hastily or leisurely as the student determines. I shall explain the methods I used and the sources I examined, in the hope that others may learn from my hard-won experience and discover for themselves the thrills, excitements and frustrations of genealogy.

I
Oral tradition

Oral tradition, that is to say information or stories handed on by word of mouth, is the starting point for all genealogists. Logically, of course, one should obtain one's own birth certificate and proceed from there, but fortunately this is rarely necessary as most of us know something, however little, of our parents and grandparents. The first step, then, is to write down everything that is known about one's family, with particular reference to places and dates, although the latter have usually been forgotten more easily than the former. When this has been done, it is important to visit any elderly relatives who may still be alive and persuade them to remember all they can. Little inducement is needed as a rule for most old people welcome the chance to talk of the past with someone who is really interested.

I was particularly lucky in this respect, as I had several relations who had reached their eighties or nineties without loss of memory or vigour. Three of my four grandparents I had known well, although they all died before I had begun my search and I shall regret to my dying day that I did not listen to them more attentively or ask more probing questions. Nevertheless, when I came to set it all down, I was pleased to discover that there was much of interest.

My first source was my maternal grandmother, a gentle old lady who died in her late seventies. She frequently told three stories of her own grandmother, whose maiden or christian names, however, were never mentioned. Only once did she remark that her married name was Allday, a providentially unusual one for which I was now duly grateful, for of all the obstacles which face the potential genealogist, the names

Smith, Jones and Brown are probably the most formidable.

This great-great-grandmother was left an orphan at an early age and went to live with her Aunt Wolfe at Tutbury in Staffordshire. She was a very strict and rather snobbish person who controlled her ward's activities closely. So when the butcher's son came courting, the lady was scandalized and forbade her niece to have anything to do with him. But love found a way, as it usually does, and the young girl, only sixteen years old, climbed the apple tree in the garden to talk to her sweetheart over the wall. Soon realizing that there was no hope of her guardian's approval, the couple eloped secretly to Tamworth, where they were married. The bride left her home in such haste that beyond the clothes she stood up in, she took to the wedding only 'a spare pair of silk stockings and her best umbrella'.

After the ceremony, Mr and Mrs Allday went to live in Birmingham, where they opened a butcher's shop in Deritend. Shortly after moving in, my great-great-grandmother spoke quite innocently to a young man in the street outside the shop, with her long hair hanging down her back. To her surprise and alarm, her husband, when he saw what she was doing, came out and was extremely annoyed. Finally, after seeing her perplexity, he realized she did not understand the cause of his anger and explained. It appeared that it was the custom then for wives to keep their hair covered in public; only unmarried girls showed their single status by letting it hang over their shoulders without hat or bonnet.

The third story about Mrs Allday was very different from the first two and possibly apocryphal. Nevertheless, it was always told to me as established fact. When still a recent bride she met a gipsy who, naturally, told fortunes. This one, though, did not speak but instead bent down and drew the outlines of seven coffins in the dust. What the poor woman thought of this macabre warning I never learnt, but it was always solemnly averred that her first seven children died young.

The only other thing I ever learnt about Mrs Allday was that she eventually had a daughter called Sarah who grew up to marry a Samuel Bull and thus became the mother of Mary Bull, my own grandmother.

Mary's husband, Rowland Wood, I remember most clearly of my grandparents, for he did not die until I was in my mid-twenties. Like so many of his generation, he was conscious of the vast changes that had come about in his lifetime. He had begun life as a farmer's boy earning £5 a year with his keep and as a young man he had attended the Straw Fair in Tutbury, where men in want of employment wore a piece of straw in their hat until such time as they had found an employer. He was very fond of reminiscing about his youth but almost the only reference I remember him making to his family was an oft-repeated remark that his grandmother had been left a widow with eleven children and had then married a widower with eleven children, so that 'all twenty-four sat down together to the wedding breakfast!'

When I began to put all this down, I was able to discover a few more things about the Wood family from two of my grandfather's sisters. The eldest daughter, Ellen, lived until she was 102 and Kate, the youngest, is still alive at the time of writing, nearly ninety-eight and in the best of health. Their mother had died young but their father, Samuel Wood, loomed large in both their recollections. After the death of his wife the younger children were brought up by Ellen, no light task for a girl of twenty. Great-grandfather frequently came home drunk late at night, when the effects of drink brought out an unwonted piety, normally absent from his character. He would rouse the entire family from their beds, assemble them downstairs and lead them in a spirited rendering of hymns from the Sankey and Moody hymnbook, interspersed by fervent and no doubt incoherent prayers.

He was by trade, at various times, a farmer, butcher and drover, one of those who herded the cattle from Derbyshire to Birmingham in two days, spending the intervening night under a convenient hedge with the cows penned in a nearby field. Certainly, all those who remembered him did so with some sense of awe. Without ever striking any of them, he ruled his family as a martinet and the only photograph I have of him bears out this impression of a stern and formidable old man (see opposite p. 49).

These, then, were nearly all the facts I could collect about my mother's parents and I set them out thus, omitting, for the time being, all brothers, sisters and cousins, but adding such dates as anyone could remember:

```
Mr and Mrs Allday
        |
    Sarah  = Samuel Bull        Samuel Wood = Sarah Marler
   d. 1929   d. 1915             d. 1914        d. 1878
              |                     |
            Mary        =        Rowland
          1874-1950     |        1871-1953
                       Ada
                   (my mother)
```

It all seemed rather sparse, but at least it was more than I could find out about my father's family, the male line of the Abbotts. Neither my father nor I remembered our respective paternal grandparents and all contact with relatives in Norfolk had been lost long ago, after my grandfather moved to Birmingham. Indeed, practically all I was able to find out about my great-grandfather was that his name was Jesse, that he had married a Sarah Dyball, that he was a fairly wealthy grocer or auctioneer and that he and his wife always had their meals in a separate room from the children. It also appeared that one son had been christened Campbell, after the Liberal politician Campbell-Bannerman, and another had gone through life with the imposing name of Oliver Cromwell Abbott! Even with this last fascinating piece of information, it hardly seemed an adequate basis for a detailed family history and looked very unpromising when written down:

```
Jesse Abbott = Sarah Dyball
        |
   Alexander
   1865-1931
        |
  John Vincent
   (my father)
```

In fact, this lack of information about the male line was one reason why I decided to study the families of all four grandparents, as far back as there was anything beyond mere names and dates to discover.

The other reason was more positive. My father's mother's name was Ridley and at one time she had proudly claimed descent from the Protestant martyr, Nicholas Ridley. When it was pointed out to her, rather unkindly, that the Bishop had been celibate, she altered this slightly to make him a colla-

16

teral ancestor. Although this belief was undocumented, we did, as I mentioned earlier, possess a family tree. It had come by devious routes from a distant cousin of my father's, who was long since dead, and it was marred by two large gaps where

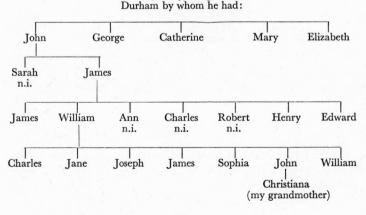

Ridley

The ancient family of Ridley has long been resident
in the county of Northumberland, as appears from divers
ancient records. The principal seat was at Willimoteswick
(nr. Haltwhistle) which with the estate was lost in Charles
1st's reign. Of the Ridleys of Willimoteswick
was Sir Thomas Ridley, Kt. who was
nt Bennett's Church, London. (He married
and heiress of William Boleyn. From the
s born Anne Boleyn, mother of Quee
at Parkend, Hexham, was until
the Ridleys of Ticket from w
Suffolk who held it to the
again become the property
Thomas Ridley. Nicholas
the ancestor of the
dley of Ridley, 1440
S. Musgrave of
Bryan Ridley of
shire, 1160. Sir
Chief Justice
the original
other Sir Thomas
settled at
estates till
adherence to
of Parkend
Esq. of Willimot
Commonwealth in
d 1680 Dorothy, dau
and left two daughters
John Ridley of Parkend
Susannah, daughter of Nicholas
and by her he had a son
second, Mary, daughter of
Durham by whom he had:

| John | George | Catherine | Mary | Elizabeth |

| Sarah n.i. | James |

| James | William | Ann n.i. | Charles n.i. | Robert n.i. | Henry | Edward |

| Charles | Jane | Joseph | James | Sophia | John | William |

Christiana
(my grandmother)

the paper had been torn away. I had often, as a child, glanced briefly at this tantalizing document without any emotion other than bafflement. It is on page 17.

The last named John Ridley was, of course, my father's maternal grandfather and he remembered him with affection and even recalled his wife's maiden name, Selina Hawkes. She was the daughter of Joseph Hawkes, a gaoler in Warwick prison, and she had always maintained that a condemned prisoner, to whom she had often taken meals, was the repentant criminal who had inspired Charles Reade to write his then famous novel *It is Never Too Late to Mend*. One minor mystery surrounded her, for no one in the family ever knew her age: a secret the old lady guarded closely.

John Ridley himself was known to my father as a happy but rather erratic individual. He changed his jobs and his address with unusual frequency and he had cheerfully enjoyed more than one bequest and as cheerfully endured more than one bankruptcy. His early life was obscure, although he certainly ran away to sea as the proverbial cabin boy, for his sea chest is still in existence.

These, then, were the beginnings of my projected family history:

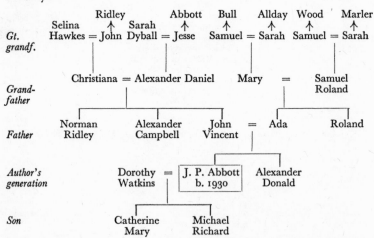

Could I put flesh on the bare bones and was there more to be discovered, I wondered. My next move was to go to Somerset House.

2

Somerset House

Somerset House or, more correctly, the General Register Office, must be one of the few places that really are unique in the true sense of that often misused word. One imagines an enormous building covering many acres, for it houses the birth, marriage and death certificates of all residents of England and Wales who have been born, married or who have died since August 1837. Surprisingly, the building, though outwardly impressive, is only moderate in size. The certificates themselves, or rather the copies, are kept out of sight in basements accessible only to officials and it is to the indexes that the inquirer must turn.

These are large, heavy, leather-covered volumes stretching endlessly along the miles of shelving which line the walls from floor to roof. The three main sections are separate and each is divided up by narrow balconies. Along the balustrades is a sloping shelf, on which the weighty books may be rested and opened. Each section begins in 1837 and runs chronologically up to the present day, every year being divided into four quarters. Unfortunately, even each quarter contains more items than one book can hold so there is usually a further division of two or three, arranged this time alphabetically. Thus, every year can necessitate the use of about twelve volumes and this means there must be around five thousand indexes in the three sections. And, of course, the number increases continually, year by year.

Apart from the names and dates, the three types of certificate, coloured pink, green and black respectively, give the following main items of information:

Birth: Place; father's name and occupation; mother's
            name and maiden name.
Marriage: Place; occupation, age, residence and literacy of
            both partners; both fathers' names and occupa-
            tion.
Death: Place; age; occupation; cause of death.

I decided that I would start by trying to find the marriage
certificates of my four sets of great-grandparents, since I was
lucky enough to know their names already. If I had not been
able to find this out, I should have had to obtain them from
my grandparents' birth certificates. As this was unnecessary, I
started on my search for the four weddings: Abbott–Dyball,
Wood–Marler, Ridley–Hawkes and Bull–Allday. The snag
was that in no case had I any idea when or where these weddings had taken place, and this could have brought me to a full
stop but for the double checking which is possible with
marriages alone.

After filling in four search forms and paying my fee at the
desk, I started, as a guess, with the first quarter of 1851 and
worked forward in time. Almost at once I struck lucky. In the
April–June section for 1852, at the very beginning of the first
alphabetical volume, I found the name of Jesse Abbott followed by the place—Norwich—and a reference number. I
had to remember that there might be more than one Jesse
Abbott of Norwich, unlikely though this might be, and that it
would be better to check straight away. Pausing only to ad-
mire the beautiful copperplate handwriting of the Victorian
clerk who had compiled this particular volume, I searched for
and found the name of Sarah Dyball, also of Norwich and followed by the same reference number. I entered this hastily on
my search form and carried on until I had found the other
three, the latest being that of Sarah Allday and Samuel Bull
in 1862.

The forms were then handed in and the fee for the certificates paid. (Nowadays there is only one fee, all-inclusive, if you
conduct your own research. Naturally, it is rather more expensive if you write in and leave the search to the official
staff.) The certificates are not produced immediately and, unless collected personally the following day, are sent by post. I

waited impatiently for a few days and when the long, official envelope finally arrived, I opened it with a feeling of expectation.

I knew now the approximate places and dates of the ceremonies and it was the final column of each certificate that drew my eye; the names and professions of the fathers of both bride and groom. Sarah Allday's father was given as Adam Allday—butcher; I had been correctly informed about his trade and now I knew his first name. Of the others, two were of special interest. The wealthy and respected tradesman, Jesse Abbott, was the son of William Abbott, a bricklayer, and he was married to the daughter of 'Daniel Dyball—gentleman'. Seldom, I thought, can Victorian England have seen these two occupations juxtaposed on a marriage certificate! At least it explained where the money came from.

The other one that took my attention was that of John Ridley. He was aged twenty-two and his bride thirty; no wonder she had never told even her daughters of her age! My first concern was to know the name of John's father, of course, and there it was: William Vincent Ridley—surgeon. This agreed with the family tree so far, although it was plain William there. Oddly enough, my own father's name is Vincent and I wondered if this could be more than just coincidence.

By now, the expense was beginning to mount and I decided that while I would still look for information about Woods, Bulls and Alldays, particularly with a view to substantiating some of those stories, it must be the Ridleys and Abbotts on which I should concentrate.

It would be one step further back if I could have the birth certificates of Jesse Abbott and John Ridley. The former, if the age on his marriage certificate was correct, had been born in 1826, long before Somerset House started, so there was no hope in that direction. John Ridley, on the other hand, by the same token must have been born in 1838 or thereabouts. The records of those first few years are not as comprehensive as they became later, so I knew I might still be unlucky.

One thing I could do to check, though, and this I did. I wrote off for John Ridley's death certificate, having found out from an old diary of my father's that he had died in January 1918, in Birmingham. When this arrived I was astonished to discover that he was then only seventy-four! This meant that he was not eight years younger than his bride as I had thought, but nearer fourteen! At least, though, his date of birth could be fixed at 1843 or '44 which meant that his birth certificate must certainly be available.

A little while later I was in London again and able to visit Somerset House. I felt sure of finishing this particular question now and, to be on the safe side, I looked for John Ridley in the indexes for 1842, '43 and '44. Unhappily, there were about a score of the same name and not one born in a place that seemed at all likely. The search forms which have to be completed, however, make provision for distinguishing between different possibilities. One writes down all the known details of date, parentage and place and these are compared by the officials with the information on the various certificates of that name. The more facts one already knows, the better are the chances of getting the correct certificate. As in all genealogy, of course, it is a distinct advantage to be chasing an unusual name. If anyone wishes to find the birth of William Jones, parents unspecified, date unknown and place uncertain, then he would do well to spend his money in a more profitable manner, for there is no way of differentiating between the innumerable candidates!

In my case, as I knew the approximate date together with the father's full name and occupation, I felt confident. After all, there could hardly have been two surgeons called William Vincent Ridley, each with a son called John!

It was with some surprise, therefore, that in due course I received a note informing me that in no case did the particulars I had given about the father agree with those on the various John Ridley birth certificates which I had listed as possible.

Clearly there was something mysterious here but I could not give up now. If I was to get any further, I needed to find out exactly when and where John Ridley was born, and the name of his mother, for the chain of ancestry can have no missing links.

I realized that the time had come to try a change of tactics.

3
Directories and printed sources

At this time I was no longer living in Birmingham, where I was born. However, I often returned for long visits and this enabled me to visit the Central Reference Library there. Most towns have such an institution, which supplements the normal library service by providing copies of rare and old books, local records, maps, pictures and the like. These are usually not for lending but must be consulted on the premises; a necessary precaution when such valuable and irreplaceable material is involved.

Birmingham is fortunate in possessing one of the best collections outside the British Museum. No matter what I have asked for, however old or esoteric, it has been somewhere in the miles of shelving which line the enormous vaulted reading room. Only once did they not have a book I needed, but I shall come to that in due course.

Two lines of research presented themselves at this point. First, to see if I could find the original text on which the Ridley family tree was based, and secondly, to find out if there was a reference to William Vincent Ridley—surgeon—or to any other members of his family, in a directory of some kind; anything, that is, that might lead me to where the family had lived and hence towards finding the next link in the chain.

Before visiting the Local History section for the trade directories, though, I tried a shot in the dark. Many pedigrees are published in various books, and while it might appear a lifetime's task to track down any particular one, in fact the task is made easy by a thick squat tome called *The Genealogist's Guide* (Heraldry Today, 1967) compiled by G. W. Marshall. I made haste to consult this extraordinary book which lists in alphabetical order all the surnames for which there are known pedigrees. Each name is followed by the source or sources and these range from the transactions of obscure societies and single manuscripts in the possession of the Society of Genealogists to well-known histories and reference books which are readily available in quite small libraries.

The name of Ridley gave many possible sources and the most obvious of these was that classic, *Burke's Landed Gentry*. I obtained the 1885 edition, calculating that if distant cousin Joseph had consulted the book at all, it must have been at about that time.

My surprise was matched only by my delight when I found that I had gone unerringly and fortuitously to the very passage of which I possessed a mutilated copy. When I had studied this carefully, I saw that there was only one, very important, difference. The original printed version ended the introductory passage with a reference to a John Ridley of the early eighteenth century and, after a brief mention of the five children of his second marriage, it followed the descendants of the only son of his first marriage, the heir Thomas. My own copy was identical up to this point but thereafter it followed instead the descendants of the second son, John, who did not themselves figure in *Burke's Landed Gentry*. This, then, is the full version which undoubtedly indicated an unbroken line running from the present day all the way back to 1160.

Ridley

The ancient family of Ridley has long been resident in the county of Northumberland, as appears from divers ancient records. The principal seat was at Willimoteswick (nr. Haltwhistle) which with the estate was lost in Charles Ist's reign. Of the Ridleys of Willimoteswick was Sir Thomas Ridley, Kt. who was buried in Saint Bennett's Church, London. (He married Margaret, daughter and heiress of William Boleyn. From the Boleyn family was born Anne Boleyn, mother of Queen Elizabeth.) The estate at Parkend, Hexham, was until 1560 in the possession of the Ridleys of Ticket from whom it passed to the Earls of Suffolk who held it to the beginning of 1600 when it again became the property of the Ridleys of Ticket—viz. Thomas

Ridley. Nicholas Ridley of Willimoteswick, the ancestor of the Ticket Ridleys, was son of Thomas Ridley of Ridley, 1440 by Audrey his wife, sister of Sir S. Musgrave of Musgrave and lineal descendant of Bryan Ridley of Ridley in whose possession was Ridley in Cheshire, 1160. Sir Bryan Ridley of Ridley who was Lord Chief Justice of Ireland was 9th in direct line from the original Bryan of Ridley and from Sir Bryan's brother Sir Thomas, the 6th in descent was Nicholas who settled at Willimoteswick. At that place they held large estates till 1650 when they were deprived of them for adherence to the cause of Charles Ist. Thomas Ridley Esq. of Parkend, younger brother of Musgrave Ridley Esq. of Willimoteswick whose property was forfeited to the Commonwealth in 1652, left a son, Thomas Ridley, married 1680 Dorothy, daughter of George Ridley of Gate House and left two daughters (Mary and Catherine) and one son, John Ridley of Parkend. He married first, 1731, Susannah, daughter of Nicholas Maughan Esq. of Whinetly and by her he had a son Thomas, his heir. He married, second, Mary, daughter of ? Ripon of Whasneyburn, County Durham by whom he had John, George, Catherine, Mary and Elizabeth. The son and successor, Thomas Ridley Esq. married etc. [cf. page 17.]

Elated though I was, I still found it an obscure, not to say muddled, account and even after reading through the turgid and repetitious sentences several times, the matter seemed very little clearer. Still, it was a promising start, if nothing more, and I put it aside while I went to consult the directories.

These were popular productions from the early part of the last century onwards and they usually cover only one town or county, listing tradesmen, professional people and gentry, each under their appropriate heading. County registers are sometimes subdivided into villages or districts, which is often a help. There are also similar works which deal on a national basis with one particular profession or calling. A well known example of these is the famous *Crockford's Clerical Directory* (O.U.P.) of the present day, which lists all clergymen.

Two others which are sometimes very helpful to the genealogist are the *Alumni Cantabrigienses* and its Oxford equivalent which list, with biographical notes, all the undergraduates of our two oldest universities from Tudor to modern times. These modern publications are in most collections of reference books but those printed in the last century are naturally available only in record offices and the larger reference libraries.

I first consulted trade directories for Birmingham for years around the early part of the last century. In the list of butchers for 1839 I came upon Adam Allday of High Street, Deritend, by his address quite certainly the great-great-grandfather who objected to his wife's unrestrained hair. There were many other butchers of that name, including even one woman, all possibly descended from some remote Allday who had first brought his trade to Birmingham.

But as it was William Vincent Ridley I was mainly concerned with, I found some old national registers of doctors and surgeons to look through. None of them yielded any result though, and I returned home no nearer to tracing the elusive physician. On impulse, I wrote to the British Medical Association and to the Royal College of Surgeons and both were good enough to check their records for me. Both, also, returned the same answer; to the best of their knowledge there never had been any member of either profession of that name.

By now, it must be admitted, I was becoming distinctly irritated by my great-grandfather's mendacity. I could hardly expect him to have considered the problems of a future genealogist, but such a blatant disregard for the truth was, I felt, quite uncalled for!

I was not able to visit the library again for some time but my father, ever willing to humour me, went himself to search, arguing that if William Vincent Ridley was not a surgeon then, obviously, he must have been something else and might yet be found in some list or other. He obtained a few local trade directories and looked for William under any and every heading which seemed even remotely possible, but still without any success. He did find a chemist called Henry Ridley living at Hockley Hill, Birmingham in 1860 and it seemed possible that he was William's brother, as shown on the family tree. Still looking at random he tried the directories for Warwickshire and at last felt that he was on the verge of discovering the first real clue. At Atherstone, a small market town about twenty miles from Birmingham, for the year 1845 was listed Ann Ridley, grocer, chemist and druggist. In 1884 there appeared Sophia Ridley, confectioner, also of Atherstone. Both these ladies appeared in the family tree and the latter was my father's own great aunt, whom he remembered.

When he wrote to tell me of his finds, I knew at once that I had the lead I needed and my next move was plain.

But I was not yet finished with trade directories. I was able to visit Lichfield and asked at the local library there if they had one which included Tutbury for the 1830s. They had; and two more tiny pieces of the jigsaw fell into place. In 1834 there was listed a John Wolfe, headmaster of an academy in Monk Street, and a Charles Allday, butcher of Duke Street, evidently the uncle and father-in-law of my eloping ancestress. And as the two streets ran alongside for some distance, the garden of the academy may well have been separated from that of the butcher's shop by only a single wall, easily overlooked by someone climbing a convenient apple tree!

4
Census returns

In 1801 the Government carried out the first national census in this country and thereafter repeated the exercise every ten years with increasing complexity of detail. The first four returns were destroyed after the results had been collated, but the subsequent ones of 1841, 1851 and 1861 were retained and are now kept in the Public Record Office in London. These are freely available to students and members of the public alike, although increasing demand, combined with limited reading-room space, make it advisable to write beforehand, when a reader's ticket may also be obtained by completing an application form. Alternatively, if it is not possible to visit the Record Office oneself, there are professionals who will undertake such research for very reasonable fees. The staff of the Record Office will provide the names of such people who are known to them, although naturally they can accept no responsibility for whatever arrangements are made. It is advisable, of course, to state the maximum you are prepared to pay, as charges are determined by the length of time a particular search takes and this in turn depends on the information you can supply. Obviously a person can be found far more quickly if his address is known than if a whole township has to be combed.

The returns, consisting of long lists of names divided into separate households, are all kept in innumerable notebooks, carefully handwritten by the clerks after the census takers had returned from their weary round of questioning. It is these same notebooks, each dealing with a separate parish or locality, which are disinterred from their subterranean hiding place for the benefit of the curious and the inquisitive.

No census, however, is made public until everyone listed is presumed to be dead and that means, in practice, that an exact century must elapse before they may be consulted. At the time of writing, therefore, it is only the 1841, '51 and '61 censuses with which we are concerned.

In 1841, ages were given only to the nearest five years, while personal relationships were not stated and are sometimes not very clear. In addition, adults had to state their occupations and a final question was put to everyone, 'Were you born in this county?' and the answer to this was either a plain affirmative or negative. Perhaps needless to say, when the answer is 'Yes', the genealogist's first reaction is one of relief, for one of his most difficult tasks is that of tracing the movements of families who were not content to remain near the homes of their forefathers. If the answer is 'No', then the record of that person's birth or baptism must be sought literally anywhere else in the entire country; a daunting, not to say impossible task in many cases. Fortunately, two things mitigate this rather depressing conclusion. The first is that, until about a hundred years ago, the modern trend towards easy and frequent migration had not yet begun; most people remained in the same area where their ancestors had lived since time immemorial. To this day, in fact, many villages have inhabitants with unusual names which can be found in the very earliest local records, and it can be plausibly argued that in some cases the population has received little fresh blood since the first Saxon settlement.

The second factor which helps us is more important, since it affected everyone alive a hundred years or more ago. In the 1851 and 1861 censuses, which are very similar to each other, ages were supposed to be correct and relationships between individuals in a particular household were clearly stated. Above all, and it is this which gladdens the hearts of genealogists, the final question was amended to read, 'Where were you born?' and as this information usually carries one back to the days before frequent movement was common, it can be invaluable.

Normally, it is the bridegroom's residence, as given on the marriage certificate, which leads to the correct census return, but in my case this approach did not work. John Ridley, married in 1860, apparently moved on almost immediately; while

Jesse Abbott, married in 1852, had not been at the same address a year earlier. This much I had already discovered.

Still concentrating on Abbotts and Ridleys, however, I decided to look up Atherstone in 1841 and 1851, and Worstead, Norfolk, in 1861. The latter place was where my grandfather, Daniel Abbott, was born, as I knew from his birth certificate, and I hoped the result would lead me to his father (Jesse)'s birthplace. It was Atherstone I was most interested in, however, and there, for the year 1841, I at last found Filliam Vincent Ridley. As I had suspected, he was not a surgeon, but a chemist, druggist and oil-and-colour man, like so many other members of the family. He was aged about forty at the time, as was his wife, Dorothy, and to the final question they had both returned the dreaded 'No'. There was also a Henry Ridley listed, another chemist aged about twenty-five, and this must have been the same that my father had already found nearly twenty years later in the Birmingham trade directory.

I went in haste to the 1851 census but I was not unduly surprised to find that by that date both William and his wife had evidently died, for the younger children, including John, were in the care of the oldest brother and sister, Charles and Jane, while Henry had moved elsewhere. I was thus no nearer to finding whence the Ridleys came to Warwickshire, save that I could now be sure it was from some other county. The information I obtained did, however, at last enable me to obtain John Ridley's birth certificate. It was in the local registrar's office and, through some very rare oversight, a copy had never been forwarded to Somerset House. Still, this cleared up the mystery of his birth and showed that he was born in August 1842 and was thus nearly eighteen when he was married and seventy-five, not seventy-four, when he died. Subsequent research has shown that it is quite common for ages to be recorded inaccurately and I suppose he can hardly be blamed for the mistake on his death certificate! I could also absolve him from wilfully misstating his father's profession. After all, he was only a young child when his parents died and may well have been genuinely mistaken, particularly as the lines of professional demarcation were drawn less clearly then than now.

William's wife, Dorothy, was shown by her son's birth certificate to have been a Marlow before she was married and both my father and I were reminded, regretfully, of two old oil paintings which had belonged to my grandmother and which we had parted with when she died. They each portrayed a rather stern, elderly lady with dark hair worn in the tight ringlets of early Victorian fashion, and although known to be an Aunt Jane and Aunt Elizabeth, were usually referred to, collectively, as 'The Marlow Aunts'.

While still wondering which way to turn next, I suddenly remembered Henry Ridley, chemist at various times in both Atherstone and Birmingham. If he still resided at 107 Hockley Hill, Birmingham, in 1861, then his answer to the final question in the census of that year should show where he and his brother William were born.

My good luck held and this proved to be the case. He had been born in the village of Sheepy Magna in Leicestershire and it was there I knew I must journey for my next step.

I had still to check up on the Abbotts, though, and here I met with complete failure. Jesse Abbott had indeed been living in Worstead at the time of the census, but on the day itself he had taken his wife and older children on a visit, leaving his youngest son and daughter in the care of two servants. Presumably he and his wife are listed somewhere in those comprehensive notebooks as visitors in someone else's house, but exactly where I have never discovered.

I also sought for and found Woods, Bulls and Alldays in the census returns and these enabled me to add the names of various brothers and sisters, as well as to fill in some other details of dates and ages. It was the entries concerning the Alldays which particularly interested me, though, and they fitted in with a later discovery to confirm or support two of the old stories. Adam's wife was called Ann and the 1861 census showed her to have been left a widow with three children before she was forty-four.

Last of all, I found my grandfather's grandmother, Sarah Marler, together with ten children and presumably still capable of bearing the eleventh. Her first husband's death and her subsequent marriage to the widower with another eleven children, if it ever happened, had yet to be proved.

5
Parish registers

It was in the year 1538 that Thomas Cromwell was first responsible for the rule that clergy should keep a register of all the baptisms, marriages and burials which were performed in their particular parish. Many years were to pass before this was general practice, for at first there was much disquiet over a system which could, it was felt, be perverted to help in the collection of taxes.

It is only partly for this reason, however, that so few churches today possess registers going back this far. Many of the early registers have been lost through the ravages of damp, fire, destruction or plain ignorance and this sad tale of neglect has persisted even up to the present century when these irreplaceable records have still occasionally disappeared. I know of one parish where the very oldest were burnt by the churchwarden because, to quote his daughter, 'He couldn't read them!' At another church, for some mysterious reason, they were thrown into an old well when it was filled in. And during the last war, of course, a few were destroyed in the bombing.

Fortunately, such acts of damage and vandalism are now extremely rare and the majority of churches have registers which cover the last three hundred years or so. In addition, some have been collected in by County Record Offices where they are looked after with the care they need and deserve. This method is not without its dangers, as Irish genealogists discovered to their dismay when the registers of Eire's churches were gathered together for safe keeping in one building. Shortly afterwards this was burned to the ground, together with all its contents, during the Troubles.

Nowadays, also, many church registers have been copied and indexed, while the modern tendency is to make photostat or microfilm copies of them. Despite such care and attention, though, it is surprising to find how many churches still possess their own books, uncopied and unphotographed, tucked away untidily in damp cupboards and largely disregarded.

They are fascinating reading in themselves, these records, even if they were not such marvellous sources for genealogy and social history alike. As one turns the thick parchment pages one finds surprising diversity, even in a single volume. The writing can be clear and neat or faded and illegible; the information can be scanty or profuse; the arrangement orderly or chaotic. The only general rule which seems to apply, and it is by no means absolute, is that the later the register, the more accurate, detailed and neater it tends to be.

Always, too, one comes upon odd snippets of fascinating information, such as was contained in the registers of Lowick in Northamptonshire where it is recorded: 'Robert Smith made Widow Alderman most miserable. January 8th, 1733.' Was she jilted at the altar? And why was the entry put in with the marriages and baptisms? We do not know.

Another unusual entry was in the records of Tutbury in Staffordshire where I once came upon an unfortunate girl whose parents, anxious to confer distinction I suppose, had insisted on having her christened Reboynerburilanor; a name which they must have dreamed up themselves.

A bizarre fact was contained in the laconic burial entry from Minety in Wiltshire which stated that 'He was the first in wool'. The significance of this is that in order to help the sheep farmers, it had just been made obligatory for shrouds to be of wool, rather than the accustomed linen.

At Minety also, almost until within living memory, there frequently appears in the registers the girl's name Friswith. This is pure Anglo-Saxon and it seems to be a genuine and lonely survivor from the remote past before the Normans imposed their own christian names upon the native population.

Sometimes the entries are pathetic and even tragic; paupers' and children's burials abound, the latter sometimes followed within a few days by that of the mother. Many bastards are recorded, although 'base born' is the more usual description of illegitimate births, while closer inspection can reveal shotgun marriages and large families where all too often few of the children grew up to be parents themselves. These are the stark, cardinal features of life and death expressed in a few brief lines which, for most people, are all the legacy they have left to posterity. 'The short and simple annals of the poor,' as Thomas Gray says.

It is to be feared that many parish clergy, even until quite recently, took the task of compiling their registers very lightly. Mistakes and omissions occur occasionally and where the exact format was unspecified, all too often the absolute minimum was written down. Some vicars, it would seem, kept rough notes and from these they periodically brought their books up to date; a method which did not make for precision. One parish in Leicestershire, for example, has many pages written not only in the same handwriting, but with the same pen and ink. Obviously, the rector or curate spent several hours one night completing his long-overdue homework!

Despite all this, parish registers provide the best, and often the only, genealogical source available for the years before 1837, when Somerset House first opened its doors. Roman Catholic and Nonconformist churches kept their own records, too, but very often these have been collected in and must be consulted in a department of Somerset House.

All three types of entries in registers are of value to genealogists, but the most important are the baptisms. Usually this ceremony was performed within a few days of birth, although adult baptisms were not unknown.

At their best, these entries can include the date of baptism, date of birth, father's full name and occupation and the mother's christian and maiden names. At their worst there is only the date and name; no more. Most fall between these two extremes and, as I said before, the tendency is for the later entries to be the more detailed. Marriages, as today, were by banns or licence and these additional records are also often available and can provide more information. The entries usually give the names of both partners, together with their parish and condition (bachelor, widow, etc.) but, like the baptisms, the details vary. The common practice, as in modern times, was for a couple to be married in the wife's parish, though not necessarily in the church, for weddings were mostly celebrated at the porch years ago. Burial entries are generally the most brief, rarely giving more than the name and date. The only other facts sometimes given are the date of death, occupation, any relevant relationship and the age. This last, which allows the date of birth to be ascertained, is infuriatingly absent from most early registers and makes these records, though useful, less valuable than the other two.

The time had now come for me to carry my own search into the churches. Logically, I should have gone straight to the Ridleys, as the Abbotts would have to be followed to Norfolk and this was out of the question for the time being. However, before I went to Sheepy Magna, there was one other entry which I was particularly anxious to find, despite the fact that it was as far from the direct male line as it was possible to go, being my mother's, mother's, mother's, mother's wedding.

I telephoned the vicar of Tamworth, who agreed to let me look through his marriage registers in a few days' time. I had, of course, very little idea when the wedding had taken place and I was rather taken aback to see how thick the volumes were. Most villages did well if they had a dozen marriages in a year, but Tamworth, a busy market town, was better patronized. It took me nearly an hour but eventually I found it: 9 December 1833. 'Adam Allday, bachelor of this parish' (a temporary address, presumably) married 'Ann Austin, spinster, of the parish of Tutbury', by licence. The couple had both signed the register, proof of a literacy which was often absent at that date when many people could indicate their consent only with a witnessed cross.

It was an odd sensation to look at the two signatures, scarcely faded after nearly a century and a half during which no one, perhaps, had ever given the lines more than a casual glance. Two things were now apparent. If her age had been correctly given in the census (I subsequently checked this against her baptism—it was true) then my great-great-grandmother had indeed been only sixteen when she eloped: a proof of the accuracy of oral tradition. Furthermore, I already knew that the first of the three surviving children of the marriage was born in 1840 or 1841, eight years later. I did not expect to authenticate the story of the seven coffins, but at least there was ample time for seven miscarriages or still-births to occur if the warning had really been given.

This diversion completed, I contacted the rector of Sheepy Magna, who said I could visit the church to inspect the registers one afternoon. I called first at the rectory, where some of the later registers were kept, and browsing idly through them I came quite by chance upon the burials of William Vincent Ridley and his wife in January 1846 and January 1848, aged forty-five and forty-seven respectively, and also of other members of the family. The registers were unusual in showing that, although more than one had died at a distance, all had wished to be buried in this their birthplace.

My main interest was in the early registers, of course, and these were kept in the church itself, in the vestry. Almost at once I found William's baptism and thereby the full name of his father: 19 March 1801, son of James Francis Edward Ridley and Jane, his wife. This showed that he was not, in fact, forty-five at his death, but forty-four; another example of Ridley miscalculation! His father's name on the family tree was simply James and the full name seemed vaguely familiar in some way. Still, the time at my disposal was limited so I was forced to skip backwards through the pages much faster than I would have liked, making a brief note of all the Ridley entries which caught my eye. There were obviously several gaps and omissions due to my haste, but by the end of the afternoon the main outline was clear. James, in his turn, was the son of John and Ann Ridley, who had been married on 24 January 1739, Ann's maiden name being Vincent. Their eldest son had been christened Vincent Ridley and the name has continued in the family for over two hundred years, as far as my own father.

Three mysteries now confronted me. The John Ridley of *Burke's Landed Gentry* could not possibly have been the John Ridley of Sheepy Magna, since the former was born after 1731 and the latter was married in 1739. To this day I do not know whether the family tree was a hoax or a genuine mistake. I am inclined to the latter, on the whole, as it seems likely that Cousin Joseph knew of his descent from a John Ridley, possibly from some other source now lost, and identified him with his namesake in the *Landed Gentry* without further investigation. All this was very disappointing, particularly as there were no Ridley entries earlier than 1739.

Of the other two puzzles, one concerned a burial in June 1739, for it was that of 'Sarah, wife of John Ridley'. How, then, could he possibly have married Ann Vincent in January of that same year? Not unnaturally, this worried me for some time until I found the simple explanation. Up to 1752, each year, for legal and ecclesiastical purposes, began on 25 March, Lady Day. June 1739 came before January 1739, which we should now consider 1740, and all was clear. John Ridley came to Sheepy with his first wife, Sarah, who died childless shortly after their arrival. Seven months later he married Ann Vincent, by whom he had more than one child.

The third and last point baffled me for much longer, though it proved ultimately to be of great interest. In 1756 was recorded the burial of one Sobieski Ridley. No relationship, no age, no further details. But why a Polish first name? It all seemed so unlikely in an obscure, eighteenth-century Leicestershire village!

6
Bishop's Transcripts

Although my Ridley genealogy had now been confirmed in outline, save for that vital mistake, there were many gaps I wished to fill in. This would require a far more leisurely examination of the records than was possible at Sheepy and I decided to try the Leicestershire Record Office. Nearly all counties now have their own record offices and here are deposited all forms of record which are of local, rather than national, interest. Very often these include the Bishop's Transcripts, which are contemporary copies of the parish registers sent each year by the parish clergy to the bishop of their diocese. In theory, these are exactly the same as the registers, but in practice there are often slight differences. Usually, the transcripts tend to be less detailed than the originals but sometimes the reverse is true, possibly because of the habit of copying from rough notes, to which I have alluded before. At all events, they provide a most valuable supplement to the parish registers and in many cases, where these have been lost, they provide the only source.

I confirmed that the Bishop's Transcripts for Sheepy Magna were in existence and in the keeping of the Leicestershire Record Office and during my next holiday I travelled to Leicester, where the thick bundle of parchments, all shapes and sizes, was readily made available. This time I went through most carefully, for there was no need for haste, and everything fell neatly and tidily into place. So attached to Sheepy were the Ridleys that they rarely went anywhere else to be baptized, buried or married, which made my task very easy. John Ridley had had seven children (see Appendix 4 for complete pedigree) and they included not only James Francis

Edward, but also a Charles Edward, a Clementina and a Maria Sobieski. As I read these exotic names, light dawned and I realized their significance.

In 1688, as everyone knows, the Catholic James II was deposed in favour of his Protestant son-in-law and daughter, William and Mary. They were succeeded by Mary's sister, Anne, and when she died the Hanoverian George was invited to England, to be succeeded in turn by his son and great-grandson, George II and George III. James II, however, had a son, known to history as the Old Pretender, who never renounced his claim to be the rightful king of England. He invaded Scotland in 1715, as did his son, the Young Pretender, in 1745. Both attempts failed disastrously and the cause of the Jacobites, as supporters of the exiled Stuarts were called, never recovered. To have supported actively either insurrection was treason, with all the hideous penalties this entailed. Passive support of the Stuarts, though not treasonable, still required considerable bravery. It is precisely this which is indicated by the children's peculiar names, for the full name of the Old Pretender was James Francis Edward Stuart; his wife was the Polish princess, Maria Clementina Sobieski, and his son, the Young Pretender, Charles Edward Stuart. The Ridleys were not alone in their defiance, of course, and the provocative names are found elsewhere. However, I understand Sobieski to be unique, even among other Jacobite families.

John Ridley, it now appeared, was a wealthy gentleman who died in 1786, his age not being stated, unfortunately. His wife, Ann, survived until 1798, having seen no fewer than six of her seven children die before her, mostly when very young. Only the youngest, James, married and had several children himself. He died in 1814 and I was able to read his will, which was also in the possession of the Leicestershire Record Office. He styled himself 'Gentleman' and was clearly still wealthy. I say 'still' for his will shows debts amounting to £1400, no inconsiderable sum in those days. What remained, though still quite substantial, had to be shared out among nine children and so nearly all of them left Sheepy to earn their livings elsewhere. My father can remember only one remark his mother ever made about her grandfather, William, who died twenty years before she was born, and this was that he was the first of the family, for several generations, to actually work for his living. It would seem that this tiny scrap of tradition was substantially correct!

It was a pity that there was no trace of John Ridley's will, which might have cast light on his origins, and the Leicestershire indexes showed that there were no local wills of any Ridley earlier than the eighteenth century. As I now knew the family to have been wealthy, this complete absence of wills surely indicated what I had long suspected: that the Ridleys originated elsewhere, probably in the north of England, where the name is far from uncommon.

Record offices shed their light in many directions, though, and a few more dark corners were illumined for me before I was finished. Among the Sheepy Magna papers was a map of the Ridley estate which was issued when the land was finally put up for auction in 1854. Why it should have been this particular year I do not know, for no one died then and the only member of the family living in Sheepy whom I could find in a trade directory was William Vincent's brother Edward, a farmer and maltster, who was still living in the village long afterwards.

The elder John Ridley's oldest son was a John Vincent Ridley and his burial entry showed him to have been ordained. There is no contemporary list of clergymen but a card index compiled by the record office revealed that he had signed the registers of Aston Flamville and Twycross as a curate at various times. Both these places are near Sheepy and I suppose he could have remained at home while still attending to his pastoral duties. Few clergy of his time were overworked by modern standards! Maybe the reason for this lack of regular employment was constant ill health, for he died unmarried at the age of forty, a year before his father. His name is also included in the *Alumni Cantabrigienses*, which shows that he attended Emmanuel College but makes no mention of his subsequent career. It gave me one other new fact, though, for which I was grateful: his father's occupation is given as a mercer, an occupation not inconsistent with the status of a gentleman.

I tried other local records, however, with less success. The county newspaper of the time contained no Ridley obituaries and the few references therein to Sheepy Magna would seem to show that John played little part in local affairs. His son James was rather more active and I found his signature attached to some of the parish accounts.

Before James reached the end of his life, the cause of Jacobitism had disappeared for ever with the death of Bonnie Prince Charlie's only brother in 1801. There were no heirs to carry on the struggle and even the Ridleys had to accept the legitimacy of the reigning dynasty eventually.

The new loyalty was demonstrated in their old manner in 1837, when the latest of William Vincent Ridley's daughters was baptized Victoria. One cannot help but wonder what her great-grandfather would have thought!

7
The Society of Genealogists

The Society of Genealogists has its headquarters in a large, converted London mansion. Membership of the society is open to anyone who is interested and willing to pay the moderate subscription. If one does not wish to join permanently, then all the facilities of the library and the various collections can be used on payment of a small fee for each day or half-day.

The society possesses, of course, all the standard works on genealogy and many of the rarer books also. In addition, there are many printed copies of parish and other registers which have been laboriously copied in freehand by conscientious enthusiasts. Card indexes of various sorts abound while esoteric publications by long-defunct associations lie cheek-by-jowl with lists of monumental inscriptions or county histories. Through the arcades of shelving the searchers pursue their quest in dutiful silence, finding their way by the duplicated guide which is available, together with many other useful publications, from the desk at the entrance.

Following these directions carefully, I found my way to the room where the copies of parish registers are kept and there, in the Norfolk section, were seven neatly typed and indexed copies of Norwich registers. Knowing that there are over thirty parishes in the city itself, I did not expect to find anything, particularly as it was largely surmise which led me there. Jesse Abbott was married in Norwich but he did not live there afterwards and, for all I knew to the contrary, he might have been born in King's Lynn or Caister, or even in another county altogether. I was lucky, though, and the indexes saved laborious checking through the pages. Jesse's baptism was in the parish of St James on 1 September 1826, and his mother's name was Ann *née* Whall, a most unusual surname. Further search soon showed that far from being an only child, as my father had always thought, Jesse was in fact one of thirteen children: the largest family I had discovered to date and only one of whom died young.

His father, William, I now saw, had died in 1847 and I could therefore expect no help in finding his birthplace from the 1851 census.

One odd thing about the many Abbott entries in St James's parish was the variation in the spelling of the surname, for I found it written with either a single or a double 't' or with an additional 's'. This was explained when I turned to the next register copy, that of St Helen's. Here was the marriage of William with Ann Whall, on 13 October 1811. The name was written as Abbett and I could only conclude it was the result of illiteracy and consequent reliance on the spelling, and hearing, of the officiating clergyman. This suspicion was confirmed when I discovered later that both partners had signed the original registers with the traditional 'x'.

After such a good start, it was a disappointment to find that the other Norwich registers took me no further. The name of Abbott occurred right back to Elizabethan times but it was evidently far from common and my next essay in this direction would have to await a visit to Norwich itself.

Meanwhile, the Ridley tree still held one gap, and that I now hoped to fill. William Ridley's wife was Dorothy Marlow, of course, but when or where they were married I had never yet discovered, for it was certainly neither at Sheepy nor even at Atherstone, whose registers I had recently examined. I turned, therefore, to Boyd's Marriage Index, a unique possession of the Society of Genealogists. This is situated in one of the larger rooms, a series of typed volumes covering several English counties. Although not by any means exhaustive, this can provide the vital clue when the vexed problem of locating a wedding comes up. Each book contains a list of names arranged in alphabetical order, each name being preceded by the year and followed by the partner and the parish. Further details must then be sought from the actual registers themselves.

Even those counties covered by the Marriage Index do not have every parish included and, except perhaps in the 'Miscellaneous' section, there are many counties not yet represented at all. Nevertheless, it has given invaluable assistance to many searchers. I, alas, was not to be one of them. I looked for William Vincent Ridley under several counties and I even tried John Ridley, in the hope of finding his first marriage with the mysterious Sarah, but it was in vain.

Other lines of research suggested themselves and I spent some time leafing through card indexes, looking for evidence of wills and peering at lists of marriage licences. For Abbotts and Ridleys alike, it proved fruitless. Finally, I went to the room at the top of the house, on the second floor. Here was an enormous collection of cardboard boxes arranged on bookshelves and labelled alphabetically. In these boxes, I knew from my guidebook, were envelopes containing all the pedigrees of various families which had been compiled, collected or discovered by members of the society over many years. Indeed, anyone who works out his family tree for himself should send a copy to the society to add to their collection.

Many genealogists have both begun and finished their search in this same room, for it can easily happen that an unknown great-uncle or second cousin has completed the task already. More usually, a person traces his own pedigree back as far as he can, and then grafts it, as it were, on to a longer and more detailed genealogical tree which has been compiled previously.

In the envelope marked 'Abbott' there were several such pedigrees but, as I had expected, none which could possibly have any connection with mine. I tried the Ridleys next. The envelope contained one or two pedigrees and also a collection of Ridley entries from various parish registers. Here and there were a few John Ridleys, but not one which could have been my fourth great-grandfather of Sheepy.

And that seemed to be that, until I remembered that I had only reached the Ridleys through the female line and that what has been done once may be done again. I put the envelope back in the box and replaced it on the shelf before moving almost to the end of the row, where I found what I was after: an envelope labelled Vincent.

44

It contained a most beautifully designed and printed family tree, about 30 inches by 24, commencing in the Middle Ages and continuing until the last descendants in the female line became Croxalls and Tongues towards the end of Victoria's reign. It was an Ann Vincent of the eighteenth century that I was after, though, and there she was: Ann, baptized at Ravenstone in 1715 and married to John Ridley of Sheepy in 1739. None of the children was listed, however, simply a downward pointing arrow to indicate that the line of descent continued. She was an only child, it now appeared, and her father, one William Vincent, had not married until he was fifty. I was fascinated to learn, from a brief note on the pedigree, that he had been a non-juror, one of those unfortunate clergymen who remained loyal to the Stuart cause and refused to take an oath of allegiance to the Hanoverian kings. They were deprived of their livings and many suffered in other ways because of their open defiance of the new dynasty. Many people shared their principles but few their resolution. I wondered now if William had influenced his daughter and how far the splendid array of Jacobite names bestowed on Ann's children was the result of her upbringing. All in all, William seemed to be a most interesting character and I hoped that I might be able to find out more about him.

Above William, the line continued back for nearly a dozen generations through a Richard Vincent, 'slain by Henry Killigrew' in 1434, to one Sir Thomas Vincent of Swinford in Leicestershire, whose coat-of-arms was a blue shield with three silver four-leaved clovers (azure three quatrefoils argent).

The whole pedigree had been compiled by a Reginald Stewart Boddington, who had appended one or two footnotes. One of these in particular attracted my attention; it referred anyone who was interested to Nichols's *History of the County of Leicester*. This I resolved to consult.

Meanwhile, there was no need, fortunately, to take elaborate and time-consuming notes of all this. The Society of Genealogists made a photocopy of the whole document for a very reasonable charge and I returned home pleased with my latest acquisition.

8
Heralds and heraldry

During the Middle Ages the heralds were the genealogists of the rich, the royal and the powerful. They were professionals; men employed by the King and nobility to understand and expound the vast and complicated network of kinship which linked family to family and generation to generation. But all the care and attention to detail which they brought so meticulously to their task was intended only for the upper classes of England and for the very practical purpose of giving legal validity and framework to their power, inheritance and alliances.

This was all symbolized by the growth of heraldry, which flourished from the twelfth century onwards. Each knight bore on his shield or surcoat a design of beast, flower or abstract shape, which he alone was entitled to use and which his sons and grandsons inherited from him in due time. These distinctive blazons, or coats-of-arms as they are usually called now, were simple at first but became increasingly complex as more and more people rose in status to claim the privilege.

Originally, the right to bear these arms was assumed but soon it became a coveted and restricted honour, marking out the proud possessor and his family as being literally armigerous, that is, qualified to bear arms. In practice this meant all members of that upper class which comprised everyone from a simple knight up to the King himself.

The privilege was not conferred lightly and, after the very early days, those who assumed a coat-of-arms, be it that of another family or of their own devising, could be compelled to discard it and even punished. The usage varied at different times. If a man died without heirs, then his coat-of-arms passed into oblivion; no one else could normally use it thereafter. Frequently, a man left only daughters who could not, in theory, bear the arms themselves. They were therefore styled heraldic heiresses and in this event their husbands took the arms by courtesy and the children of the marriage by right. Otherwise the privilege could be inherited only in the strict male line.

Many books have been written about the science of heraldry and it would not be relevant to deal with the matter at any length here. Briefly and basically, there are two metals in heraldry: gold and silver, often depicted by yellow and white, and referred to in the Norman French of heraldic language as 'or' and 'argent'. There are also five basic colours: black (sable), blue (azure), red (gules), green (vert) and purple (purpure), although the last two are very uncommon. (The terms, incidentally, are pronounced in the English manner.) Any coat-of-arms must be represented by metal on a coloured background or by a colour on a gold or silver background. A colour must never touch another colour, in other words, nor a metal touch another metal. The reason for this rule is simply to ensure clarity, for a black lion on a blue field, for example, would be indistinguishable at a distance.

In describing a blazon the field, or background, is given first. Thus, to take an example known to everyone, the flag of St George, ascribed to the warrior saint by credulous medieval heralds, is 'argent a cross gules' or to put it in plain English, 'on a white background, a red cross'.

In addition to the basic coat-of-arms, there is also a crest, which was originally worn on the helmet and should always be so represented, and the badge which could be worn either by a lord himself or by his retainers and servants. Sometimes, but certainly not always, these two could be the same. Heraldry is often confused, while inaccuracies and inconsistencies abound.

Coats-of-arms were originally displayed only on shields and banners, but soon spread to the surcoat and other items of the knight's equipment and thence to civilian clothing and in due course to book-plates, coach doors and many other places. Each coat-of-arms is unique. At any one time only one person may use a particular blazon; even younger brothers should introduce some slight mark of difference, although this rule seems to be observed less frequently nowadays. Above all, a coat-of-arms is a possession, to be used and passed on to one's heirs like any material object. It is this which links heraldry so closely to genealogy and led the first practitioners of the former craft to become experts at the latter, for it was in order to safeguard and check this complex system that the heralds existed. In the early days they presided at tournaments and knew by heart the blazon and lineage of all possible contenders, whom they marshalled and proclaimed. Later, King Richard III established them in the College of Arms, where they assembled an impressive collection of records. Periodically, until the end of the seventeenth century, the heralds would also carry out a 'Visitation' of each county, when the qualifications of all gentlemen using coats-of-arms were politely checked, recorded and, all being satisfactory, approved.

Since 1682 the heralds have no longer conducted these Visitations but they continue their work of regulation; registering successful claimants to ancient coats-of-arms, designing or approving new ones and keeping a watchful eye generally on modern heraldry, which shows no signs of dying just yet. Naturally, genealogy is a vital part of their work and their archives, which are not open to the public, contain many family secrets. They will undertake genealogical research for anyone but, as specialists, they charge high fees and are not likely to be in a position to help anyone of plebeian birth.

However, there are many people in England today who do not know that they are entitled to use a particular coat-of-arms. The discovery or proof of this right can be an additional aim of the genealogist, for it is not sufficient merely to have the same name as an armigerous family. I myself have absolutely no right whatsoever to use the Abbott coat-of-arms, a very beautiful one incorporating three golden pears, which belongs to another family altogether.

Like other people, though, I may have inherited one or more through the female line, as both my Ridley grandmother and my Vincent fourth great-grandmother had no brothers and were therefore heraldic heiresses.

In the past, when matters were more flexible, many of the

SHEPEY, N.E.

Sheepy Church and rectory, c. 1770. Bottom right—the Vincent coat of arms and crest.

Joseph Hawkes (the gaoler of 'It is never too late to mend'). This illustration shows how the record of a really old daguerrotype may be preserved by rephotographing the original.

Sam Wood is affectionately remembered for his piety and hymn-singing when in his cups!

Abbott family group, 1881. From left to right (top), Alexander, William, Henry, Edward, Beatrice; (centre) Lilla, Sarah, Jesse, Frances; (bottom) Campbell, Lewis, Oliver.

heralds' records were made available and appeared in various publications. When I came to consult Nichols's *History of Leicestershire,* I saw at once that it was from the College of Heralds that the Vincent pedigree had originated.

9
The Vincents

The pedigree of Vincent of Sheepy was originally compiled by Augustine Vincent, himself a member of both the family and the College of Arms, for whom he undertook the Visitation of 1619. It was extended during the next Visitation of 1682 and subsequently found its way to John Nichols, who incorporated it into his monumental *History of Leicestershire* with a few additions which he garnered himself from sundry parish registers.

Reginald Stewart Boddington, whoever he was, had presumably taken this as his framework and then extended it by personal research, but as most of his own work covered only the nineteenth century, long after Ann's time, it had little relevance for me. The original, in fact, proved to be of much greater interest, for several reasons. (See Appendix 4.) Firstly, it began two generations earlier, with a Miles Vincent who had owned lands at Swinford in 1317 and whose son John, the father of Sir Thomas Vincent, had been appointed receiver of King Edward III's revenues in Ponthieu in 1330. Unhappily, his mathematical skills seem to have been no better than those of his remote Ridley descendants, for he was imprisoned in the Tower of London in 1337 until such time as he was able to settle his accounts to the King's satisfaction.

Sir Thomas, the third generation, had married Joan Bernake, the daughter and heiress of another local knight while their only son, another John, had married Margaret, the daughter of Sir Baldwin de Drayton of Cranford. I had already decided that my eventual aim would be to get back as far as the Norman Conquest if at all possible, as this is the ambition of most genealogists. It might be feasible to do this by going through the female line yet again, I thought, and finding out about the Drayton ancestors of this Margaret, who were eventually also my own.

In the meantime, it was towards William Vincent, the father of Ann and my fifth great-grandfather, that my attention turned. The note by his name merely repeated what I already knew: that he was a student of Emmanuel College, Cambridge, where he obtained his B.A. in 1684 at the age of twenty; that he married a Mary Twinbury in 1714 and that he had been a rector of Ibstock about 1699 but had been ejected as a non-juror. This was all I could have expected and I never supposed that any scrap of gossip or reminiscence concerning someone so distant would ever reach me. I was wrong, though, for John Nichols had written his book around 1811 and he had talked with local people whose memories had retained the stories told by their parents, which bridged the gap of nearly three-quarters of a century. One of these informants was the rector, Thomas Fell, whose father had held the position before him and who had lived in the parish since boyhood. From him, and from a distant relation who was Dean of Westminster, John Nichols had assembled what information he could gather about William Vincent and presented it as a detailed footnote. I quote it in full:

This William Vincent, a celebrated Non-Juror, was called Blofferby Will from his residence at Blackfordby (commonly now named Blofferby), a hamlet of Ashby-de-la-Zouche, and probably officiating in the chapel there after his ejectment from the rectory of Ibstock. He was for some time a resident at Ravenstone in that neighbourhood. On this, Mr. Fell remarks, 'William Vincent certainly was a Non-Juror, but that Blofferby was the benefice from which he was ejected I am not so sure. His cousin at Sheepy afforded him an asylum, and maintained his daughter, Mrs. Ridley, till she married, and when I was a child, I remember to have heard her say, that the garret in which our men servants slept was the room in which her father lived and died. She was born at Ravenstone'—to which the Dean of Westminster adds, 'William Vincent, rector of Ibstock, must be the Blofferby Will and Non-Juror. I have heard that he was a worthy man, and nominated by the Pretender to a Bishopric. No wonder that he was a Non-Juror, for the whole family were high Tories, not to say Jacobites, and so was nearly the whole county. His daughter, Ann Ridley and her husband I remember: Ann I saw in extreme old age in 1794; and before that at Sheepy in 1757, when I heard her talk of her father William.'

This was probably my most exciting discovery of all. Suddenly, through the mists of two centuries, my ancestor became alive for me; a brave, upright and unyielding man, possibly bitter and unforgiving, for unlike many of the other non-jurors who lost their comfortable livings, he had no private income to make his sacrifice only a gesture. His refusal to compromise earned him a life of poverty during which he pinned his hopes, political and personal, on the possibility of the Stuarts returning. In the event, his life was dedicated to failure and the only saving feature, his courage apart, is that he did not live to hear of the final disaster at Culloden.

If I do not read too much from the brief lines of John Nichols, he was respected rather than loved, and his affections were reserved for the child of his late marriage. Ann was twenty-five when he died and she never forgot either his example or his teaching. Even when the cause of the Stuarts was clearly lost for ever, she continued doggedly to proclaim her loyalty by the names she gave to her children. One effect of her convictions is with us to the present day. Every generation of boys, for over two hundred years, has included a Vincent in their number: an unknowing tribute by posterity.

Since then I have tried, without much success, to find out more about William Vincent. One thing is certain: he was never rector of Ibstock. At that time this parish was in the diocese of Lincoln and the church and diocesan records tell the same story: in 1699 the then rector, Edmund Lees, died and was succeeded by a John Laughton. It is possible that William was presented to the living at this time, then found to be unacceptable, or it may be that the patron withdrew his promise. Either way, though, William could not have legitimately styled himself rector and it seems likely that he was only a curate whose status was unintentionally exaggerated by his daughter or grandson.

I was able to check this in a book called *The Non-Jurors: Their lives, principles and writings* (John H. Overton, 1902) which includes the names of all known non-jurors compiled from contemporary lists. One entry reads '—Vincent, curate of—in the diocese of Lincoln'. This can be only William and I would give a great deal to know the full truth of the matter.

Certainly his conduct compares favourably with that of his own maternal grandfather, Francis Markham. This pliant clergyman was rector of Creaton in Northamptonshire and in 1654, as a Master of Arts of Oxford, he wrote an ode in praise of Cromwell. In 1660, at the Restoration, he retained his living and wrote another ode for the university, this time in praise of King Charles II. The Vicar of Bray, one feels, would have approved, but not William Vincent.

One other small item I discovered about William, but I shall refer to that in its proper place—the next chapter.

10

Wills and other sources

There is a variety of subsidiary sources available to the genealogist which can supplement and complement those records
already mentioned. The most important of these are wills, of
which an enormous number survive from the last thousand
years.

Wills are not left by everyone, of course, and of those which
have been written, many are now lost. No one left a will unless he or she owned property which was sufficiently valuable
to warrant some directions as to its disposal and, yet again,
many wealthy people seem to have simply not bothered.
Nevertheless, if the relevant wills do exist and can be traced,
they may provide invaluable assistance and information.

Most wills state the names and relationship of the benefi-
ciaries, usually the marriage partner and children, and also
(the original purpose, of course) the estate and possessions of
the testator. In addition, they show where the people mentioned were living and the approximate date.

It will be seen from this that the evidence of wills is contrary to that of other genealogical sources. Birth and marriage
records, whether at Somerset House or in parish registers, lead
us from an individual back to his parents; wills lead forward
from an individual to his children. Wills, therefore, for genealogical purposes, must be used differently from other sources.
Basically, if one wishes to find the father of a John Smith of
London, living around 1800, one finds all the wills for the
London area of that time which were left by people named
Smith. Then, if one finds a will mentioning a son called John,
the link has been made and another step backwards (the right
direction for genealogists!) has been taken.

The example I quote, however, will readily illustrate the troubles and difficulties of this approach. All the same, even conceding these hazards, wills are worth looking for, and it is here that the problems really begin to arise.

Since 1858, all wills have been kept at Somerset House where inspection presents no difficulty, but few people need such evidence as late as this.

For wills before then, the question of location is extremely complex. In brief, the position is this: The jurisdiction over all wills was originally entirely ecclesiastic and, after a man's death, his will was taken to the appropriate court for Probate to be granted. If proved, the will itself was retained by the court and a copy given to the executors, certified as their authorization. If a man died intestate, then the next of kin would apply to the court for letters of administration and the procedure would be very similar to that of a will.

Each court had jurisdiction over a particular area; the smallest local ones frequently being the Archdeaconry courts, to which the will of anyone owning property only in that area had to be brought. If property was owned within the jurisdiction of two or more local courts, then the matter was referred to a higher, overriding court, usually the Episcopal court. To take this a step further, if property was owned in more than one bishopric, then it was the Archbishop's Prerogative court which was responsible. Finally, if the inheritance involved was in both provinces, then the will had to be proved in the senior of the two, Canterbury.

The foregoing is only the outline, for the details, exceptions and ramifications are legion and wills were retained in many different depositories all over the country. Nowadays the position is simpler and, as a generalization, it can be stated that the wills which went through the local courts have been collected in by the county record office most nearly concerned, while those which went through the Prerogative court of the Archbishop of Canterbury (usually abbreviated to P.C.C.) are now at the Principal Probate Registry, Somerset House. Apart from these two sources, which cover the majority of cases, wills may be found in the Public Record Office, the Lambeth Palace Library and some other places. Usually there are adequate indexes to make the task of the searcher a little easier.

For a complete understanding of this intricate subject, one should consult an invaluable book entitled *Wills and their Whereabouts* by Anthony J. Camp and available from the Society of Genealogists. (See Appendix 1.)

Despite this preamble, I must confess that my own researches have benefited very little from wills. At Leicestershire, as I have already related, I was able to read the last testament of James Ridley, but there was no trace, there or elsewhere, of his father's.

Two other wills provided me with items of some interest. The copy of one I found in a book in the library of the Leicestershire Record Office; it was that of John Vincent who died in 1564, the great-great-grandfather of William. He left his lands and property to his wife, Alice, in trust for the children, but to his son Richard, then only nine years old, he bequeathed a silver goblet, twelve silver spoons and a gold ring which was obviously a family heirloom.

The other will was also that of a member of the Vincent family, but as it had been proved in the P.C.C., it is now deposited at Somerset House. This was not a direct ancestor, but another William Vincent, who was rector of Sheepy Magna and the cousin of my fifth great-grandfather. It was he who 'maintained Mrs. Ridley till she married' and lodged her father in the garret, possibly with a guilty conscience to stimulate his charity. After all, he was probably a Jacobite himself, albeit one whose self-interest had outweighed his convictions. He died only a short time before his namesake and remembered him in his will with a small bequest. The rector refers to his relation as 'my cousin William Vincent of Ibstock' and it is this brief description which provides the only contemporary evidence to support the theory that it was from Ibstock that the non-juror was ejected.

Other wills which I tried to find proved to be unobtainable or uninformative and in my search for something beyond the cold facts of birth, death and marriage, I cast about for other sources. The availability of these can depend to a large extent on the station in life of the family. Labourers and farm hands pass away with no testimony to their very existence except the brief lines of the parish register, and wealthier folk often fare no better.

I combed the Leicestershire Records Office for more knowledge about the Ridleys and the Vincents, but with little success. In the Hearth Tax of 1666, George Vincent of Sheepy paid tax on seven chimneys, more than any other local householder, and in 1563 Robert Vincent was in possession of 340 sheep, 43 cows and the first farm rollers ever recorded in Leicestershire.

I also found another mention of George Vincent, together with his brother and uncle and several other landowners of Sheepy. In 1659 they signed a legal agreement with the lord of the manor, Thomas Levinge, by which the common land was appropriated, enclosed and divided. It was a process which was taking place all over the country at this time and it often caused great hardship to the poorer folk. It was interesting to discover that in Sheepy, at all events, this was carried out in a more liberal fashion than in many places. At least three acres were allocated to each cottage 'that there might be no depopulation by reason of the said enclosure', as the document stipulated.

Finally, I left this side of my researches and turned elsewhere. One source of information for genealogists, which everyone knows about, is the family Bible. On the flyleaf of this heirloom many families have for years recorded births, deaths and marriages; in fact many Victorian Bibles had specially printed pages for just this purpose. There had been one belonging to the Abbotts, apparently, but no one will ever know if it would have proved valuable, for it was burned after the death of a great-uncle. In view of his grandfather's illiteracy, it seems likely that it was, in the context of generations, a recent acquisition.

One family Bible was still extant, though, and this belonged to my mother's family, the Woods. It was at this time in the possession of my Great Aunt Kate, my grandfather's youngest sister and rising ninety-four. She lived in Clent, in Worcestershire, and made us very welcome when we called. I had not seen Aunt Kate very often, but I was strongly reminded of her eldest sister Ellen, whom I had known well and who had died a few years before at the age of 102, the oldest inhabitant of Coventry. The whole family was well known for health and length of life, and when the Bible was produced I was pleased to see that it recorded the births of Kate and all her ten brothers and sisters, although there was no earlier information, unfortunately.

I already knew the dates when they all died and the new information from the Bible now enabled me to work out their ages. Two brothers had died when very young but of the remaining nine, one had lived to over 100, two to over ninety and five to eighty or more. (See Appendix 4.) Their total age was 788 and the average nearly eighty-eight, and even that will be increased if Aunt Kate achieves her ambition to reach the century.

All these, of course, were the children of my great-grandfather, Samuel Wood, and their longevity has always been a source of amazement to others. The longest lived of all, Aunt Ellen, always ascribed her health and vigour (she ran up and down the stairs until well after her hundredth birthday) to drinking only water. Alas for this theory, for no one else was teetotal! Sam Wood himself was a notorious toper and when taking a draught directly from the barrel was fond of declaring 'Out of the wood and into the Wood!'

Against this, I suppose Aunt Ellen would have replied that he was only eighty-three when he went and comparatively young.

While I pondered all this, wondering how far such a capacity for long life was hereditary, Aunt Kate produced a souvenir of nearly forty years past.

It was a newspaper cutting of a letter to the *Daily Mail* of 1927 and is reproduced on the following page.

This was the preceding generation and it seemed to confirm my conjecture; unless of course there was something particularly healthy about the air on the Derbyshire–Staffordshire border!

The Ann referred to was the 'Aunt Tipper' for whom my grandfather worked as a boy. He always remembered her with affection and she was certainly a sterling character, for she ran the farm herself after the death of her husband and also helped to look after her motherless nephews and nieces. She became blind in old age but managed to knit more than a

Dear Sir,

The last of a remarkably long-lived family, Mr. James Wood, of Bell House Farm, Anslow, near Burton-on-Trent, died a few days ago at the age of 90. He was one of a family of eight who were born in Hatton in Derbyshire. Their names and ages at the time of their death were:

John 97	Ellen 84
Thomas 88	Reuben 77
Mary 90	Ann 96
Samuel 83	James 90
Total 705	Average 88$\frac{1}{8}$

Yours faithfully,
George Shipton

Sycamore Farm,
Hatton,
Derbyshire.

hundred pairs of socks for the soldiers of the First World War.

The two oldest brothers, John and Thomas, had emigrated to America where both became very prosperous. It is said that, having no children of their own, they wrote home to find out the names of their prospective heirs, but some of the wealth was lost in a financial slump and the remainder was left to an adopted daughter who was required to take the name of Wood.

Of the other minor sources consulted by genealogists, the most usual are the settlement certificates which accompanied poor families when they moved into another parish, the records of apprenticeships, marriage licences and lists of electors. These are mostly in the keeping of the local county record offices and, in my experience, the archivists are very willing to advise and assist.

One approach to family history which is often forgotten is the collection of old photographs. These, like so many relics of the past, go through three stages. First, they are recent, modern and of topical interest; secondly, they are old-fashioned rubbish to be thrown away or destroyed; thirdly, they are valuable records to be preserved and cosseted. Photographs, in common with other records, rarely survive the second stage. When they do so, they should be treated as objects whose historical value will increase as time goes on.

Generally speaking, photographs became common only towards the end of the last century and wedding groups, which are particularly useful to the genealogist, were not at all common until well into the present century.

If one is lucky enough to find old snapshots, it is as well to have them rephotographed by a professional. This will guard against further deterioration and very often the quality of faded or indistinct photography can be improved by skilful treatment. I myself was lucky enough to acquire several old pictures, including an early daguerreotype of my great-great-grandfather, the gaoler of Warwick. This is very fragile and the picture under the glass is gradually disintegrating. The process cannot be indefinitely arrested but, for a few shillings, I was able to have it copied. The new photograph may not have the antique value of the original, but it is fully as accurate and will never perish.

I am also fortunate in possessing an Abbott family group of 1881, overwhelmingly Victorian in costume and posture alike, as well as portraits of all except two of my great-grandparents. These were collected from distant relatives or found in old albums stored away in cupboards and attics. It is really surprising what has lain neglected for many years in such places. From old books I have photostats of various prints, including one depicting Sheepy church and rectory as they were in William Vincent's time. One final source for genealogists, different in kind from all the rest, deserves a chapter of its own.

II

Monumental inscriptions

Tombstone, monument, plaque, gravestone, epitaph, stele or cenotaph—every variety of memorial tells us something, although the wind and rain of centuries have all too often obliterated the message.

Monumental inscriptions, as they are collectively known, have existed for countless years and, where they are protected from the weather, they survive the passage of time virtually unchanged. Outdoors, in churchyards, it is very rare to find a tombstone older than the eighteenth century; the rich were buried in vaults and the poor had nothing to mark their last resting place.

From the genealogist's point of view, the ideal epitaph gives dates, age, address, next of kin and a brief biography: a combination always sought for but rarely encountered. Nevertheless, tombstones have a fascination all of their own and many odd and bizarre facts are chronicled in stone for the diversion of posterity.

A fellow genealogist of my acquaintance claims an ancestor in Suffolk whose headstone is the only one known to be equipped with a sundial. At Malmesbury in Wiltshire is the tragic and surely unique memorial to the woman who was killed by a tiger: it escaped from a travelling menagerie. Few monuments are quite so unusual as this last one; most are touching or foreboding, such as the one in Fillongley churchyard, Warwickshire, which warns: 'Stop, look, prepare, reflect, while this you view. Who next must die uncertain. Why not you?' Or the sad memorial at Berkswell, also in Warwickshire, to the young man who died of a broken heart, aged twenty-one.

One of my favourites, at Minety in Wiltshire, commemorates Captain Andrews of the Life Guards who 'entering as a private, he by merit rose to be captain'. No small achievement in the mid-nineteenth century.

At Sheepy Magna I found the Ridley graves grouped in one corner of the churchyard and almost overgrown. They told no unusual tale and only confirmed some of the dates which I knew already. My greatest disappointment was to find John Ridley's epitaph; it consisted only of the date of burial, so my last hope of finding his age at death was gone.

My maternal grandmother's family, the Bulls, lived at Sutton-on-the-Hill in Derbyshire and in the last century census returns I had found no fewer than seventy-four people of that name living in the village and the surrounding hamlets. As they seem to have shared about half a dozen christian names among them, the picture was uncommonly perplexing!

I was not, I must admit, particularly interested in the family, for it seems likely that they had lived in the area since the Domesday Book was written, as solid, worthy countryfolk whose only marks on their little world were the well-trimmed hedges, the green fields and the harvest each autumn. All the same, I wished to find out something about them and I had known for a long time that there were many of the family buried in the churchyard there. My grandfather was never, I gather, very fond of his wife's relations and, shortly before he died, we took him for a car ride to revisit the haunts of his youth. My happiest memory of this experience is of the old man tramping round Sutton churchyard peering intently at the gravestones and finally exclaiming cheerfully, 'Well, I've outlived the lot of 'em!'

This was several years before I commenced my genealogy and I remembered no details, so I made another journey into Derbyshire. The little church with its avenue of trees is still as quiet and secluded as it was when my grandparents were married there in 1897.

The larger part of one end of the churchyard seemed to be occupied by the Bulls. They were laid in lines, almost like a huge family tree spread out on the rough turf. Closer inspection showed only twelve memorials, which included three Thomases and three Williams. Nearest the hedge was the grave of William Allday Bull, my grandmother's eldest brother. He died when only nineteen in 1887 and the headstone added 'also in memory of Annie Bull, died 16th of September, 1887, aged 17 and interred at Boston Spa, Yorkshire'.

This could only be his sister who had been in 'service' and who was so distraught when she heard of her favourite brother's death that she drowned herself. My mother remembers my grandmother talking to her sisters about 'poor Annie', but it was not until more than half a century had passed that she was finally told what had actually happened.

Alongside this stone was another pathetic grave; this one of their brother Thomas, only one year old. Like her husband, Rowland Wood, my grandmother had ten brothers and sisters, and of these, three have lived to reach their ninetieth year.

No others of my grandmother's generation are buried at Sutton, but behind her brothers' graves stand the memorials to her parents, Samuel and Sarah, and two of her uncles. Behind them again are buried Sam's parents, Thomas and Ellen, while further back still is the tombstone commemorating Thomas's parents, Charles and Elizabeth Bull, both born way back in the eighteenth century. (See Appendix 4.)

Four generations lie there and, for all I know to the contrary, another fourteen were buried when headstones and monuments were not for farmers and labourers. 'And some there be, which have no memorial', to quote Ecclesiasticus.

It was a single tombstone which provided me with my greatest surprise and my most unlikely coincidence. My maternal grandfather's grandmother was the lady who was alleged to have married the widower with eleven children after she had been left in a similar position. I had discovered that her maiden name was Shaw and that she first married a wheelwright, William Marler, and bore him the eleven children of whom one, another Sarah, subsequently married Samuel Wood and so became the mother of my grandfather. I was still searching for her second marriage and I decided to visit Hanbury in Staffordshire, where William Marler lived and worked, and where some of his descendants are still living today.

The vicar kindly allowed me to explore the registers and I soon completed the list of William and Sarah's children (see Appendix 4), which included a Drusilla, a most unusual name for countryfolk to choose at that time. I could find no trace of Sarah's second marriage, however, and if it took place at all, it must have been elsewhere. I suppose I should have finished at that point but, like most genealogists, I can rarely keep entirely to the matter in hand. So I looked further back and for 1830 I found Sarah Shaw's marriage to William Marler, where one of the witnesses was an Elizabeth Marlow. As such people were usually relatives, I assumed this to be the sister of the bridegroom, for the spelling of surnames, even by then, was still rather arbitrary. In 1806 was the baptism of Sarah Shaw, daughter of Francis and Ann; and in 1807 was the baptism of William, son of John Marler and his wife, Elah (where did that name come from?). All this fitted together very neatly, but without anything worthy of particular note, so there I let the matter rest.

Hanbury churchyard has now been cleared in the modern fashion and the church is surrounded by neat greensward, while the old tombstones are ranged round the edge, next to the wall. I walked along the line, looking casually for any inscriptions of familiar names, when I came across the gravestone of the aforementioned John Marler. He had died in December 1851, aged seventy-four, and his wife (Helah, this time!) had survived him by twenty years to become yet another of my ancestors to reach the age of ninety.

It was not these facts which took my attention, though, but one phrase on the stone which stated baldly after John Marler's name, 'A native of Sheepy, Leicestershire'. My mother's great-great-grandfather had been born in the same tiny village of Leicestershire as my father's great-grandfather! And then came another thought. William Vincent Ridley's wife, whose birthplace was so far unknown, was a Dorothy Marlow!

I hurried home to look through the photostat copies of the Sheepy registers which I possessed. On one page was a reference to an Abraham Marler, probably John's brother, and on the very next sheet the same person's name written in a different hand and spelled Abraham Marlow!

Two grand old ladies (this was taken in 1958 when Ellen on the left was 100 and Kate, still very much alive, was 86).

St James's, Old Norwich, where thirteen family baptisms took place. William Abbott lived here from 1812 to 1847 and this scene must have been a familiar sight to him.

Sam Bull, photographed in his butcher's shop by an itinerant photographer who persuaded Sam to pose as he was.

Another Abbott group, taken at Wroxham, Norfolk—a remarkably clear photograph of about 1895. The solemn expressions are the result of having to keep quite motionless during the long exposure!

It does not appear that Dorothy Marlow was born in Sheepy, but the likelihood is that she had relatives there. It is thus very probable that my paternal grandmother, born in Hull, and my maternal grandfather, born in Derbyshire, were distant cousins!

This in itself is remarkable, although I have not yet proved the actual connection, but perhaps the oddest feature is that this should have been revealed by an epitaph: a double coincidence against which the odds must be enormous.

12

The Abbotts

William Abbott, or Abbot, Abbotts or Abbett, was married in 1811 at St Helen's Church, Norwich, and died in St James's parish, also of Norwich, on 27 July 1847, aged fifty-six. This much I had discovered from the register copies in the possession of the Society of Genealogists. He was illiterate, a journeyman bricklayer, the father of thirteen children and the husband of Ann. Of his character and outlook I knew nothing, for no memory even of his existence had survived to the present generation.

In such a situation, one seizes the smallest scrap of evidence on which to build a theory. Of his wife, Ann, he seems to have been very fond. It was clearly not a shotgun wedding and not only was his first daughter called Mary Ann, but another was christened Ann and yet a third, Sarah Ann. Surely this indicates strong marital attachment? And did the names Jesse, Rachel and Isaiah mean that their parents were unusually devout? Who can tell?

Now that I knew where William had lived, however, it was possible to find him in the census returns, or at least in that for 1841. This added only two further facts to my meagre store. One was that William Abbott lived in Water Lane, a slum area described in a contemporary document as consisting of 'humble dwellings, mostly with broken windows through which could be seen caged pigeons in almost every house where many poor weavers lived.' The other was that both he and his wife stated that they had been born in Norfolk. By 1851, of course, William was dead and his death certificate showed that he had died of bronchitis after three months' illness. Ann still lived in Water Lane and the census of that year showed that she was formerly a silk loom weaver and had been born in Norwich. In 1861 Ann was still alive but now living a few streets away in Berry's Yard, alone except for her youngest daughter, Amelia.

Did she receive any support, moral or financial, from her son Jesse, at that time living in a comfortable house with at least two servants? I do not know and can only reflect that my grandfather, who was born in 1865, never mentioned his grandmother in any way and not one of his four sisters bore her name.

One other conclusion I draw from a very faint indication. There was no compulsory schooling until 1870 yet Jesse, born in 1826, could read and write, as could even his sister Rachel. Did William Abbott struggle against the lifelong poverty which must have been his lot, pinching and scraping to send his children to school? It is a possibility and I can say no more.

It seemed now that the next step would be to find William's baptism entry in the Norwich registers. He might have been born outside the city but it seemed unlikely, for his trade was that of a townsman. Unfortunately, there were more than thirty Norwich parishes at this time and only seven of their registers had been copied and indexed by the Society of Genealogists. I wrote, finally, to the Norfolk Record Office, in Norwich, and they arranged for someone to search the Bishop's Transcripts for the years around 1790. The name of Abbott is not common in Norfolk, even today, and it was unlikely that there would be more than one William born there at any one time.

I was lucky and the searcher found the entry without any difficulty, although his age at death, as in so many cases, was only approximately accurate. William was born in Saint Andrew's parish in 1788 and the record was unusually detailed: 'Born July 27th, William, son of William Abbott and Mary his wife, late M. Nook, spinster. Publicly christened 13th August.' So he had died on his birthday and his first daughter was called Mary Ann, instead of simply Ann, because that was his mother's name.

There were no other Abbott entries in that register for more than ten years either way, so I could only assume they lived in Saint Andrew's parish for a very short time.

Shortly after this discovery, my brother and I had the chance to spend two days in Norwich, an opportunity which probably would not recur for some time and of which I determined to make the best use. We were now fumbling in the dark, for we needed to find the marriage of Mary Nook to the elder William Abbott and the baptism of the latter. Unlike the succeeding generation, there could be no question of help from censuses or Somerset House and without knowing the ages of the two people concerned, or where they lived, the prospect of further progress seemed remote.

We decided to spend the entire two days in the Norfolk Record Office, from opening to closing time, examining all the Norwich registers and concentrating on the fifty or so years before 1788. Even excluding the seven parishes whose registers I had already checked, this proved to be far more difficult than we had anticipated and only by ignoring the burial entries in most cases did we manage to finish the last register before our time ran out.

It was, I suppose, a rather forlorn hope, particularly as the Norwich transcripts are divided up in an unusual fashion: into those copies which were sent to the bishop and those which were sent to the archdeacons. The former were collected only once out of every seven years and, when we visited, were still in separate bundles for each year, with all the parishes together. The latter, covering the remaining six out of seven years, were grouped in the conventional way, according to parishes. Add to this that there are some gaps and one parish not included at all, and it will be readily apparent that the task of the searcher is far from straightforward. Fortunately, the missing parish was St Helen's and this, copied and indexed, I had already inspected in the library of the Society of Genealogists.

We set to work ready to take a note of any Abbott entries and soon they began to turn up, but few in number and mostly in family groups which seemed to have no connection with our own. We also looked for the surname Nook, in the hope that it might provide a lead, but it was entirely absent.

Previously we had met four different spellings of Abbott, but now we found even more. There was Abbet, Abbots, Abot, Abbitt and even Ebbots, Ebbets and Ebbetts, all interchangeable according to the whim of the curate or rector making the entry. When the two days were over, we examined our lists ruefully. Not only was there no marriage of William Abbott and Mary Nook to be seen, but in 1771 two separate William Abbotts had been baptized. Both would have been only seventeen when the younger William was born and, even if they were not too young then to be fathers, there was no way of distinguishing between them. Closer examination, however, showed that one of these Williams had moved with his family to another parish and died when only a child.

That left the field clear for the other candidate, and the entry, if it is indeed the correct one, brings the whole family tree to an undignified and abrupt end, or rather beginning, perhaps. It was in the registers of St Stephen's parish and read simply, 'January 21st, 1771, William, son of Susan Abbott. Base.'

And there, until that elusive marriage is found or until new evidence is uncovered, the matter rests (see Appendix 4). I can never be certain whether or not this illegitimate William is indeed the father of William the bricklayer and, even if the baptism of another William turns up one day in a village outside Norwich, it will require further facts to distinguish between the two. Unhappily, William was an extremely popular name at that period.

Only the very slight hint provided by a name may support the belief that Jesse Abbott's great-grandmother was the erring Susan. He had an elder sister of that name, which was not common then, and it is at least possible that she was so named by her father after his grandmother; he certainly believed in the general principle of naming children after relations.

To all this, though, there is a postscript. Although not common, the name of Abbott occurs as far back as the sixteenth century in the Norwich registers. We have to remember that the population of England today is at least ten times what it was in the Middle Ages, so any given surname was probably ten times less frequent then than it is now. Consequently, and particularly where such sedentary people are concerned, any Abbott of six hundred years ago in Norfolk is very likely to have been at least a collateral ancestor.

I was far from genealogy, studying an entirely different matter, when I came upon my forebear, if such he was. In fourteenth-century England, the most lowly people were the serfs, men and women forbidden to leave their lord's land and subject to many galling restrictions. Almost the only way that they could become free and improve their lot was by fleeing from the manor and reaching a place where they were not known, usually the nearest town. Escape was always hazardous, however, for any fugitive who was recaptured and found guilty could be punished with extreme severity.

The manor roll of Forncett, near Norwich, dealing with complaints about such runaway serfs in the year 1373, records that 'The arrest was ordered of John Baxter of Multon and William Baxter his brother, Simon Herberd and John Abot, because they removed themselves outside the demesne.'

I like to think that this remote forefather managed to evade capture and to retain his freedom. But I shall never know.

13
The Draytons

The ultimate aim of all genealogists is to trace descent as far back as the Norman Conquest, A.D. 1066. There are very few families that can do this in the male line all the way and, in England, only two that can go further—the Ardens and the Berkeleys, who are both descended from men living in the reign of Edward the Confessor, the last Saxon king but one.

Like the vast majority of amateurs, I knew that I should have to be content with much less. Still, I would reach the Conquest somehow, if it meant going through the female line several times over. I had joined the thread of memory to the line of research, adding two generations of Abbotts to four of Ridleys and fourteen of Vincents, so to reach the eleventh century could I link with another line stretching even further? Looking at the Vincent pedigree, I saw that Sir John had married Margaret, daughter of Sir Baldwin de Drayton of Cranford. Who were the Draytons, I wondered. Perhaps this connection, tenuous though it might be, was worth investigating.

I consulted Marshall's *Genealogist's Guide* and once more in the Birmingham Reference Library I turned to Drayton. There were only a few lines and these referred me to Bridge's *History of Northamptonshire*. This was another old and heavy volume, of the kind that earnest antiquaries of the eighteenth and nineteenth centuries seem to have devoted many years of their lives to writing.

I soon uncovered a good deal of information about the Draytons (see Appendix 4), who had taken this name from their manor near Lowick in Northamptonshire. Much of the author's information, according to a footnote, came from an obscure book called *Succinct Genealogies*. When I asked for this from the reference library, they were obliged to admit defeat for the first and only time in my experience. However, they consulted a catalogue for me and I learned that the book was written in 1685 by Robert Halstead, the pen-name of Henry Mordaunt, the Earl of Peterborough. It is an account of the owners of Drayton Manor, which he wrote in collaboration with his librarian. Only twenty-four copies were printed, of which three survive, one at Drayton and two in the British Museum.

I wrote to the British Museum and after a necessary wait of some months I received for a moderate sum photostat copies of all the pages dealing with the Draytons. In the meantime I had found a few facts from the Victoria County History series, in the volume dealing with Northamptonshire.

For once I was able to follow through chronologically, instead of working backwards in the usual genealogical fashion, and I found, for the first time, distant ancestors who were actively involved in the making of history. The Draytons were Norman in origin, as I had hoped, and the first of the family was Aubrey de Vere who came to England with William the Conqueror or soon afterwards. His son and namesake was Lord Chief Justice and Chamberlain to King Henry I—the high point of the family's fortunes, apparently, although Aubrey himself was killed during a London riot in 1141. Of his two sons, the elder became Earl of Oxford and his descendants likewise, while the younger, Robert, inherited Drayton. With that genius for picking the losing side which he shared with his remote descendants, Robert fought for the Empress Maud who promised him a barony if she should obtain the crown. Perhaps needless to say, he never got it. He married a Margaret Furnell, who brought Cranford as part of her dowry, and was followed by his son, Henry, a noted warrior who was constable of the castle of Gysors in France, near which he slew a Ralph de Vaux.

His son Walter changed his name to Drayton and was also the first to adopt the family coat-of-arms 'argent, a cross engrailed gules'. This was in token of his intention to go on the Crusades when he did, in fact, accompany Richard Cœur-de-Lion, who knighted him. Sir Walter was succeeded in turn by

Henry, Baldwin, John, Simon, John and Baldwin, the last of whom married Alice de Prayers and was the father of that Margaret who wedded Sir John Vincent. The main branch of the family subsequently lost most of its property and eventually died out in the male line.

Of all the members of this family, it was Sir Simon who was the most fascinating. As my seventeenth great-grandfather (one among two hundred thousand or so), my connection with him was of the slightest. But I felt I wanted to know more about him simply because he seemed so remarkably wicked.

It was about this time that I was able to visit St Peter's church, Lowick, a beautiful building which stands where men have worshipped God for over a thousand years. The present church was largely rebuilt in the late fourteenth century by Sir Henry Green, who acquired most of the Drayton inheritance and whose splendid tomb still stands in the south chapel. A few relics of the earlier churches were incorporated by Sir Henry in his new structure and of these the most remarkable is the series of stained glass windows in the north aisle.

The style and design is of the early fourteenth century and some signs of disorder and rearrangement indicate that the glass is not in its original position and has almost certainly been transferred from an older building. Sixteen men are depicted in glowing tints of ruby, blue, green and yellow. Fifteen of these have been identified as conventional biblical characters, mostly from the Old Testament, such as Solomon, Daniel, Elijah and Jacob. It is the last figure which is puzzling: a knight wearing full armour of the late-thirteenth- or early-fourteenth-century type, with mail and long surcoat. Over his left shoulder hangs his shield, clearly emblazoned with the engrailed red cross of the Draytons and in his outstretched hands he holds the model of a church, as though making an offering. At one time this was thought to be Sir Walter, the Crusader, or even Sir Henry Green, but the style of the armour clearly rules out both and it is now generally accepted as being Sir Simon (1282–1357). But why should his likeness be portrayed in such saintly company? And what was the significance of the offered church?

By great good fortune, the rector of Lowick had recently

been in touch with Mr F. R. H. Graves, a historian who had been investigating the life of Sir Simon. When I wrote to him, he was good enough to tell me the results of his researches. These, combined with what I already knew from other sources, made up an extraordinary story. The mystery of the window portrait was explained and the darker side of the Middle Ages revealed in all its cruelty and callousness.

14
Sir Simon

Sir Simon de Drayton was a medieval knight whose vices and virtues were typical of the savage times in which he lived. He was born in about 1282, the son of Sir John de Drayton and his wife, Philippa de Arderne, and he succeeded his father when only about nine years old. He married Margaret, the daughter of Sir John de Lindsay, and by her he had a son, John, his heir, and probably other sons who figure in the pages of Sir John Froissart's *Chronicles*.

Of Sir Simon's private life nothing is known and his behaviour as a husband and father may have been exemplary. It is only from his public acts that he is known to us and it is by these that he must be judged. He became involved in turbulent events from an early age and he used his feudal powers with a disregard for legality which was unusual even in that lawless and disturbed time.

In 1313, Simon became involved in some way with the murder of Piers Gaveston, the favourite of Edward II. This probably earned him the gratitude of Queen Isabella, of whom he now became a strong supporter, and it was to her influence that he was indebted for many favours. She secured for him the post of Forester of Rockingham, probably a valuable sinecure, and helped in his appointment to various embassies.

Despite this, Sir Simon's financial position was far from satisfactory and he became heavily in debt to one Agnes de Holdenby, a moneylender of Thrapston. With characteristic impatience and ruthlessness he resolved to free himself of this burden by violent means. In 1319 he led a gang of rioters, mostly Drayton tenants, who broke into the woman's house and carried her off to Northampton, where she was secretly imprisoned without food or water for five days. It was widely known that Simon was responsible for this outrage, which made him liable to the charge of keeping a private prison, a capital offence. The Constable of Northampton ordered the arrest of Sir Simon and twenty-three others who were involved, while Lord Zouche, as the local King's Justice, set up a commission to investigate the whole business. At the same time, various local magnates searched for Agnes de Holdenby, but without success.

Sir Simon had disturbed the hornet's nest, but as he hastened to reach Queen Isabella with his own slanted version of what had happened, his followers perpetrated a final and frightful atrocity. During the second week of May the unfortunate woman was removed to Shuckburgh in Warwickshire, where Simon had family connections. There she was blinded and her tongue torn out before being 'let to go inhumanly like a beast', as the Sheriff's report put it.

Public opinion, normally tolerant of killing and robbery, was fully roused by this dreadful affair and a peer of Parliament, Hugh Audley, was appointed to adjudge the matter. Those who had actually carried out the crime were brought to trial and punished with the full rigour of the law, Sir Simon coldly abandoning them to their fate. He himself, the real culprit, somehow escaped with only nominal punishment, thanks to the Queen's influence and the fact that her lover, Mortimer, was a kinsman of Lord Zouche, himself an enemy of Audley. These fortunate circumstances did not protect Sir Simon from widespread execration and either because of this, or through genuine contrition, he performed an act of piety to expiate his guilt. This appears to have been the establishment of a private chapel with daily services of atonement. The chapel has long since disappeared but the stained glass windows in Lowick church probably originated there and the picture of Sir Simon holding out his offering is a symbol of the deed of penitence.

A year or so later, Simon was summoned to fight for the King against rebels, in the campaign which ended at the battle of Boroughbridge. He took no part in the actual battle, evidently considering that the opportunity was too good to waste. Instead, he waited until his neighbour from Orton Longville, Sir Peter Saltmarsh, had gone off loyally to fight, then attacked and pillaged his property. Simon and his Lowick tenants carried off livestock to the value of £40 and injured several servants before starting off belatedly to pursue the now vanquished rebels. Unfortunately, Peter Saltmarsh was a kinsman of the powerful D'Arcy family of Lincolnshire, who supported his case to such good effect that Sir Simon found it expedient to depart on an embassy to the Abbey of Cluny, a stratagem arranged for him by his friend Robert Baldock, an influential courtier.

In 1324, Queen Isabella went abroad and Simon accompanied her, to return in 1326 when he consented to the deposition of Edward II. A few years later he deserted the Queen's cause and helped to bring about her final downfall, choosing to forget how much he owed her. This defection, however, gained him the support of the young King Edward III, by whom he was afterwards regarded with favour.

Simon continued to play an active part in public affairs, serving in the Parliaments of 1322, 1329 and 1336. He fought in France in 1331 and also took part in campaigns against the Scots in 1315 and 1327, on the latter occasion clashing again with Sir Peter Saltmarsh and thus with his D'Arcy kinsfolk. At about this time, also, together with his son John and several others, Simon was indicted for murder, the victim being apparently a tenant of Sir Peter and named as one John of Overton Longville. Simon's luck did not desert him and although he seems to have been found guilty, yet he was saved by the King's pardon. The feud persisted for many years and even old age could not cool Sir Simon's appetite for brawling and worse. When he was over seventy years old, in 1355, the King intervened yet again, to pardon him for the murder of Sir Ralf D'Arcy.

If the King was constant in his support, it was because Sir Simon could be trusted to carry out difficult tasks with energy and loyalty, if not discretion. When the Bishop of Ely was implicated in a case of alleged murder, Simon was one of five knights appointed to the commission of inquiry. (No one, least of all Simon himself, appears to have considered this choice at all inappropriate!) Such was his diligence in this matter that both he and his colleagues were excommunicated by the Pope, a fate from which even the King's favour could not save him. But papal anger disconcerted him no more than the verdict of courts or the disapproval of neighbours and he seems to have weathered this storm as he had all the others.

Around 1344, perhaps conscious of past sins and mindful of approaching death, he gave to the prior and convent of Paventon some of his lands in Stoke-Goldington 'for the good of his Soul there to be prayed for'.

He died on 31 May 1357, aged about seventy-five and survived by his widow, Margaret.

Murder, robbery, torture, kidnapping, treason and excommunication—I wonder if anyone else has discovered an ancestor who was so consistently, thoroughly and unbelievably evil, as my remote forebear. Or is this a new and hitherto unexploited form of snobbery?

15
Loose ends

I was in St Mary's church, Warwick, admiring the most magnificent of English tombs, that of Richard de Beauchamp, Earl of Warwick, when the thought came. Selina Hawkes, my great-grandmother, was the daughter of a gaoler in Warwick prison, just down the road. Surely she must have been baptized here? Knowing as I now did that she was much older than her husband, John Ridley, I wondered if she had, in fact, misrepresented her age at marriage as much as he had. Instead of an alleged twenty-two, he had really been seventeen. She had said she was thirty. Was this really so?

I was not able to look through the registers myself, but the verger, when approached and given the details of what I wanted, agreed to look for me. When his letter arrived some days later, I was not unduly surprised to find that Selina was not born in 1830, which would have accorded with her marriage certificate, but 1827. She was thus thirty-three, nearly twice her husband's age, at the wedding and she can hardly have even met him until she was thirty or so.

This lent added poignancy to the story my father had been told about Selina's death. As she lay dying she repeatedly called out for someone called Ben, a name known to no one present; and she had no brothers. One wonders if he was a young man who jilted her before she met my great-grandfather, or if he died in the Crimea. This, at least, is one secret that no one will ever uncover.

Still seeking to place the last few pieces in the jigsaw, I wrote to Somerset House yet again. I wanted to find the marriage of Sarah Marler, widow, to an unknown widower, in an unknown place at a date later than 1851, when her first husband was still alive. It was a long shot, but the name Marler is very uncommon and Sarah Marlers were never thick on the ground, so I had hopes of success. I was not disappointed and the correct certificate duly arrived. Sarah Marler, widow, married John Wooley, widower, a painter and decorator, in St Bartholomew's church, Birmingham, on 8 November 1853. What they were doing in Birmingham I cannot say, for both bride and groom came from the same village of Hanbury in Staffordshire and had known each other since childhood. Indeed, one of John's eleven children was baptized at the same time as one of Sarah's, so the two families may well have been friendly. I can never prove that 'all twenty-four sat down together to the wedding breakfast', but I think that this at least may be accepted on trust.

One minor mystery about Sarah Shaw/Marler/Wooley still baffles me. For both her marriages she signed her name in the registers and was therefore at least partially literate. And yet, on the only birth certificate which I possess of one of her children, she signed with a cross. I don't know why and I am reluctant to accept the obvious explanation that she had broken her right wrist at the time.

I am still, to this day, searching for Ridley ancestors, but without much hope now. My John Ridley could have been born almost anywhere, and at any time between 1700 and 1720. There are many candidates and until I find one who married a Sarah and then moved house, there is no way of distinguishing among a large number of possibilities. All the published pedigrees of Ridley were examined, but to no avail. Perhaps one day either I or another of his descendants will track him down at last.

I unearthed one story about an ancestor even more distant that Sir Simon, and this by accident. When studying the Draytons I had noted, without too much interest, that Baldwin had married an Alice de Prayers. She was a descendant of one William de Prayers who, according to the terse lines of the chronicler, 'in 1192 was taken prisoner by the Saracens in the Holy Land'.

Many months later, reading a biography of King Richard Cœur-de-Lion, I came upon this William again. Richard (known to the Arabs as Malek Ric—King Richard) was hawking near Jaffa one day, accompanied only by a few knights, when he rode into a Saracen ambush which was designed to take him alive. He would have been taken without doubt, being heavily outnumbered and some of his escort slain, but for William de Prayers. Showing both presence of mind and self-sacrifice, he called out, 'Saracens, I am Malek!' and was immediately surrounded and taken prisoner. This stratagem gave Richard the chance to escape, leaving William still a captive of the no doubt infuriated Saracens.

He remained a prisoner for several months, but it is good to know that Richard, whose renowned chivalry was not always to be relied on, did not forget William. The King's last act, before sailing for home, was to ransom the man who had so gallantly saved him. It may be an indication of William's prestige that no fewer than ten Saracen nobles had to be handed over in exchange.

Sarah Dyball does not appear to have been a gentleman's daughter after all, despite the statement on her marriage certificate. When I found her baptismal record, it showed her father to have been a carpenter. Her parents died when she was young and she became the ward of a wealthy uncle, John Piggin. It was from him that the money must have come which enabled Jesse Abbott to become a prosperous businessman. When he died, his widow went to live with one of her daughters and I have been told that the poor old lady was quite incapable of even the simplest housework, as all her life she had relied on the help of servants.

Sometimes, ironically, one discovers too much, so that a plausible theory suddenly beomes untenable. When I found Ann Austin's baptism entry in the Stoke registers, I remembered that she had become an orphan at an early age, so I looked for evidence of her parents' deaths. In 1821 there was the burial of an Ellen Austin aged forty, clearly her mother. Unfortunately, three pages later in 1823 was the burial of another Ellen Austin, this time aged twenty-seven. I have still no idea which is the right one.

Occasionally, too, one finds out something which might have been better left unknown altogether. Quite recently, since beginning this book in fact, I became curious about Adam Allday's death, for his burial was not recorded in

Tutbury where he had returned with his family at some time before the census of 1851. I obtained his death certificate from Somerset House and found that he had died in a Staffordshire lunatic asylum in 1854, after three years' insanity and fifteen months' paralysis.

This in itself was an unpleasant discovery, but its implications were even more distressing. It is more than possible that before his marriage Adam had contracted syphilis, which he transmitted to his wife. Through miscarriages, still-births and early deaths this would certainly account for the loss of the seven children. Even without treatment not everyone died from the disease and Ann eventually recovered to bear healthy offspring. Adam was less fortunate and the final stage, which was incurable and could remain latent for many years, at last appeared with all its horrifying and fatal effects.

The second stage may include a transitory rash or facial markings and I cannot but wonder if the gipsy who told my great-great-grandmother's fortune so unerringly had some knowledge of this disease. Perhaps she recognized poor Ann's symptoms and knew their dreadful promise of infant mortality. The malady was far from uncommon in those days and the prophecy thus becomes a shrewd appraisal of possibilities rather than a genuine example of supernatural precognition. One wonders also if Aunt Wolfe has not been unfairly vilified to five generations of children. She may have had reasons beyond just snobbery for distrusting her ward's sweetheart.

One last story I found out from a second cousin, and it has an odd fascination for me. One of Jesse Abbott's daughters, my Great Aunt Beatrice, emigrated to Canada and married a Manitoba farmer called Stewart. One very bitter winter they sheltered a traveller who had lost his way in a blizzard. He had been recently widowed and was taking his baby son on a desperate journey in search of work. The Stewarts looked after them both until the spring, when they offered to keep the baby until the father had found a job and lodgings. The man reluctantly agreed that this was the most sensible course and he duly went on his way alone. He never returned and no word was ever received from him. His fate remained a mystery and the boy was eventually adopted by the Stewarts, who had no children of their own.

For the rest, I have conjecture, imagination and many questions. How, for example, did Jesse Abbott, the son of a poor bricklayer, manage to marry a rich man's niece, so that her money made him prosperous and well-to-do? Alas, no one now knows.

Treating my ancestors as a random sample, I draw some interesting, but possibly ill-founded, conclusions. The Norman conquest to the present day covers twenty-nine generations, an average of just over thirty-one years—rather more than one would have imagined.

It is rather humbling to remember that as most of us know five generations personally (grandparents, parents, ourselves, children and grandchildren), it requires the experience of only six selected individuals to cover nearly a millenium.

Christian names varied surprisingly little through the centuries, the two most popular ones of the past being Ann and William. Others which have never fallen out of favour are John, Robert, Mary, Richard and Margaret, with children named more often than not after parents or other relatives. The use of surnames as Christian names was widespread, particularly during the last century, and this in itself often provides the genealogist with a useful clue.

Names are not only our most personal possession and our ultimate identification as individuals; even alone and unsupported, as the next chapter shows, they can provide a window which, dim and distorting though it may be, enables us to see further back into the past than any birth certificate or parish register could do.

16

Surnames

In one small South Wales town with which I am familiar, there are today so many people with the names of Jones, Williams, Davies and Evans, that differentiating between one person and another is sometimes very difficult.

The inhabitants solve this problem with characteristic Welsh ingenuity, bestowing on the people concerned allusive nicknames derived from their particular attributes or occupations. So there is Tom the Oil, Morgan the Milk, Evans the Bank, Powell the Bakehouse and even Phil Brass Band and Phil D.C.M. (a veteran of the First World War).

This is the result of a growing population with too many people sharing too few names and it is a modern repetition of a practice which prevailed in England up to six hundred years or so ago, and in Wales until rather later.

In most small communities people were known only by their christian names, each person having one only and this sufficing for all purposes. It was not long, though, before numbers increased to the point where this lack of variety caused difficulties of identification. The problem was overcome when most people began to acquire temporary nicknames— temporary, that is, in the sense that they were not normally inherited. Thus the John who cut and sewed cloth was universally known as John Taylor, the Sam with fair hair became Sam Whitehead, John the son of John was simply John Johnson and the William who lived near the wood could be referred to as William At-the-Wood, or just William Wood.

These names, or by-names as they are generally termed nowadays, were apparently bestowed in an arbitrary fashion, but retained by a person all his life and used in the manorial rolls or other official documents. This fashion, cumbersome but picturesque, endured for more than a hundred years after the Norman Conquest, but in a society based on the hereditary principle it could not last.

The change which provided us with our modern surnames came about around the thirteenth and fourteenth centuries and it was a process which is still not fully understood. About then, the exact time varying considerably with different areas, ranks and individuals, these by-names became hereditary. For the first time, Edward, son of John Taylor, became Edward Taylor, even if he were a farmer or butcher. Similarly, John Short's son Harry, even if he were six feet or more in height, remained Harry Short, while Jack Williamson's children stayed as Williamson and never became Jackson. Why people were not just referred to by their parentage as, say, Paul the son of Peter, and why this change should have come about in such a comparatively short time, is rather a mystery. One possible explanation is that few Saxon names survived the Conquest, when the English mostly adopted the names brought over by the Normans, which were part of the common heritage of European Christendom. There were probably not so many of these available and a few were very popular. Hence the chances of more than one person having the same name were very much increased.

The fact that this new system did arise is a great help to the social historian, for it freezes for us the society of that time in an unchanging pattern. Thus the surname Grocer does not exist today, for in those days his trade was run by the Spicer. Henryson is rarely if ever a surname, for Henry originates from the French; the English version was Harry, so Harrison is well known today.

The vital part played in the medieval economy by the Smith is shown by the extreme frequency of this name today, when the actual trade has almost disappeared. Each name tells a story. Even if we did not know it from the history books, we could tell which was the supreme weapon of the period. There is no Loader, Musketeer or Rifleman, but Archers, Fletchers and Bowyers are common.

Medieval England was richly endowed with animals and birds which have nearly all followed the mammoth into extinction by now. We can see that the Elephant, Monkey and Tiger were unknown, but the Wolf, Wildboar, Otter, Eagle, Hawk, Buck, Bear, Heron and Roe must have been an everyday sight to our forefathers, for all occur as surnames today.

There is no legal obligation for anybody, man or woman, to take their father's name, or even their mother's. A man may assume any name he likes; even deed-poll is simply the optional registration of an established fact. He may also change his new name as often as he wishes, providing that he does not thereby evade any legal or financial obligation. It is only by such wilful misrepresentation for an illegal purpose that anyone can be prosecuted for not using their usual name.

The habit of centuries is now so strong, however, that in the overwhelming majority of cases, people use their parents' names without question. It is this custom which tells each of us one tiny fact about an ancestor who was remote when the Tudor priests were reluctantly opening the first pages of their newly instituted parish registers.

Some completely new names have entered the English language within the last five hundred years. These are mostly foreign names, brought across the narrow seas by immigrants and distorted by time, accent, illiteracy and unfamiliarity.

Apart from such as these, all English surnames can be divided very neatly into four categories, according to their different derivations. They are as follows:

1. *Place names* This is possibly the largest group of all, and it covers all those names which were first applied to people who lived in or near a particular place. We have Grove, Wood, Forest, Street, Field and Meadows, whose dwelling places were obvious. There are also Newbury, Cornwall, Carlisle, Lincoln, Hampshire, York or Bristol, whose names refer to a place of origin. Obviously no one living in the capital would have been called William London, but he might well have become that if he had moved into a distant village. The rather odd result of this is that Scotts, for example, are more common in England than Scotland, the minority having presumably returned to the land of their fathers. The Englands of England must have similarly moved out and then in again. Sometimes names were taken from obscure villages or ham-

86

lets which no longer exist, and this makes for confusion. More often, those called Sutton have no possible way of knowing which of the numerous Suttons their ancestors came from. The same insoluble problem confronts Nortons, Eastons, Oakleys, Hamptons, Bradleys and many more.

In my own case, I do know which Ridley is intended, for it was from the village of that name in Cheshire that Bryan, the first of the family, took his name before his descendants moved north. Drayton, too, is a name which clearly derives from the manor near Lowick and it is more than possible the other Draytons in the country gave their name to other families.

2. *Occupation names* This is also a very large group and it includes nearly all the trades, positions and occupations which existed in the early Middle Ages. Apart from the ones I quoted earlier, there are Farmer, Butcher, Tanner, Cooper, Baker, Miller, Shepherd, Fisher and a host of others. It must not be supposed, though, that Bishop, Monk and Deacon indicate descent from someone in holy orders. After all, surnames began when clerical celibacy was the rule and any such paternity would reflect little credit on the founder of the family! In a similar way, King, Duke and Earl do not, I'm afraid, show noble ancestry. All these names indicate either that their first owners worked for the person referred to or, more likely, the name properly belongs to the next group.

3. *Nicknames* This is a smaller group than the first two, but it is in many ways the most interesting. It consists of those which originated as by-names describing appearance, character or disposition but which became hereditary and were often applied as surnames to people who in no way merited the epithet. It also includes what at first sight appear to be occupational names. So Bishop could be someone who had played the part of that dignitary in the local miracle play; King could have been an authoritarian or overbearing person; Monk someone of unusually devout habits (or the extreme opposite—our ancestors had unsophisticated senses of humour!). Alternatively the latter could have returned to the world after his novitiate without taking his final vows, in which case his name should perhaps be in the preceding group. A nice point!

87

My own name of Abbott is generally considered to belong to this group and my ancestor may either have portrayed an Abbot in some revels or else bore the name because of a resemblance, real or fancied, to the head of the local monastery! Most names of this type, though, are more obviously derived from nicknames. There is Black, for someone who is dark; Little, for someone who is small or, humorously, very tall; Whitehead is fair-haired; Jolly, Pretty, Coward, Gay, Armstrong, Swift and Hardy are all self-evident.

The aforementioned names of Bull, Heron, Wolf and others derived from bird and beast, belong here and most refer to some peculiar physical or mental characteristic of the first person to be so called.

4. *Patronymics* This last group covers all names which derive immediately from the first possessor's father. Peter, the son of Sam, was Peter Samson, but his own son Peter became Peter Samson too, instead of Peter Peterson. Johns is really John's, the son of John. Robinson is Robin's son and James is the same with the final apostrophe and 's' forgotten. Many christian names, which are also surnames, have lost the possessive form over the years, but their origin is still the same. Thomas, Henry, Francis and Samuel join with Peters, Humphreys, Jackson, Watson and Thompson as surnames which were originally the christian name of someone's father.

It happens occasionally that names in this group originate from the mother rather than the father, although this is less frequent than might be supposed. Margery's son becomes Margerison, but Nelson can be either from Nell's son or from Neil's son, and Shirley, for example, derives from the place of that name rather than from a person.

These, then, are the four groups, and all English names, however twisted, changed or corrupted by time, fall into one of the categories, even if there is some overlap as in the case I quoted. Surnames differ from christian names in that they are virtually never invented or improvised. Unlike Wendy, Florence, Dawn, Rock, Errol and Elvis, they are not the creations of yesterday, but the only heirlooms possessed by everyone and handed down for perhaps twenty generations.

In Appendix 2 I have included a list of the most common names, in order of frequency. It should be remembered that this includes both England and Wales and is thus affected by the fact that the Welsh have fewer names than the English and so have to use each one more often.

Which is where we came in!

17
The English overseas

The modern upsurge of interest in genealogy, which is so evident in England, is more than equalled in America and the Dominions, where many people have strong emotional and ancestral ties with this country. Many overseas visitors, in fact, come here to see the homes of their forebears and, if possible, to find out more of their family history.

For those whose families moved abroad recently the problems are no different from normal, but for those whose forefathers emigrated some time ago, research must begin on home ground before the trail can be followed back to this country. Occasionally, visitors have the idea that London contains records from the entire Commonwealth and omit the essential first steps which must be taken before they come here. Not all, it is true, have such faith as the American who contacted a professional genealogist of my acquaintance. He had no idea, apparently, where or when his English grandfather had been born, but he enclosed the old man's photograph as a suitable starting place for research!

Fortunately, such clutching at straws is unnecessary for most people. Of course, for those whose ancestors have lived in America or the Dominions for many generations, the pursuit of genealogy presents problems which are outside the scope of this book. However, the number of Americans who can genuinely trace descent from one of the Pilgrim Fathers is very limited and, in fact, the majority of US citizens are probably no more than fourth or fifth generation Americans. It has been calculated, for instance, that between the years 1770 and 1890, more than ten million emigrants crossed the Atlantic, from whom must be descended many times that number. As a similar influx took place in what are now the Dominions, for most genealogists of English stock it requires only a few backward steps before the trail returns to the home country.

Surprisingly, such overseas genealogists are very often much better catered for than those of us at home, for the compulsory registration of births, marriages and deaths in their countries often includes far more detail than is demanded in Britain.

In Tasmania, for instance, at the end of the last century, even the death certificate had to include such unlikely details of the subject as the length of residence in the country, place of birth and age when married. With such a wealth of information, the task of the searcher is certainly made easy.

It is difficult to give individual details for all parts of the Commonwealth, for in many large countries the arrangements vary from one state to another. In addition, changes of régime are not infrequent in some parts of the world, with consequent changes of regulation, storage or emphasis. Her Majesty's Stationery Office tries hard to keep up with the fluctuating patterns and has produced various editions of a booklet called *Abstract of Arrangements Respecting Registration of Births, Marriages and Deaths in the United Kingdom and Other Countries of the British Commonwealth of Nations and in the Irish Republic.* This should be consulted by anyone who is seriously interested, but I have included some of the more salient facts in Appendix 3.

In America, the situation is even more complex and the student is advised to consult the local city hall, for the storage and regulation of records vary widely from one state to another. It can be safely assumed, though, that the registration of births, marriages and deaths has been universal for many years. Also, America has conducted her own censuses for an even longer time than has this country.

The first of these was in 1790 and like our own they were repeated every ten years, with variations. Unlike our own, these records are still extant from the very beginning, even though at first only the head of each household was recorded by name, all other persons in the house being entered simply as either a male or female of a particular age group.

From 1850 onwards all inhabitants were named and, in a

similar manner to our own census, everyone had to give their state or country of origin. In 1880, the last census which is available for public examination at the moment, a further step was taken and all those listed had to name the state or country where their parents were born.

Nearly all these census returns are available in the National Archives, Washington, D.C., and many have been copied for various libraries and other public institutions. Unfortunately, the returns are divided up into counties or city wards and are not usually indexed or listed alphabetically, so that prolonged research may be necessary to find a particular family or individual.

It is clear from the foregoing, therefore, that most Anglo-Saxons overseas are very recent emigrants, historically speaking, and that very little difficulty should be experienced in tracing back the three, four or five generations which are all that have intervened since the family left England.

Having traced his family back to the original emigrant, the great problem confronting the Englishman overseas is to know whereabouts in this country he should begin further research, and it is this question of location, as always, which is crucial. To know that one is descended from, say, a William Smith who arrived in Australia around 1835 from an unknown place in England is simply not sufficient by itself to make further progress at all likely. The area of search must be narrowed down, preferably in time and certainly in space. Happily, there are several ways in which this may be done.

First, as always, it is of great help to have an unusual name, not only because this means that there is less chance of confusion, but because even today, after centuries of mixing, many names are far more common in certain parts of the country than they are in others. Everyone knows that a Rhys or a Morgan is likely to be of Welsh origin, but these are only two of the most obvious examples. I have lived recently in both Nottinghamshire and Wiltshire. In the former county I met the fairly common names of Hallam, Clipstone, Brailsford and Wass, which I had never even heard of previously. In the latter, there were Telling, Ponting, Cove and others which are unusual elsewhere. Many books have been written about the origin of surnames and many of these have lists showing where these names are most prevalent.

The name of Fox, for example, is found most frequently in the north, particularly Yorkshire, while the extremely rare Weatherhog occurs almost exclusively in Lincolnshire. Of other names, Watkins is most common in the Welsh Marches, Belcher in the West Country, Rump in Norfolk and Sillitoe in Yorkshire. If a specialist book on surnames does not help, then recourse to the various volumes of the Post Office Telephone Directory, to be found in any public library, may provide a useful indication. It must not be forgotten, however, that the rules about distribution do not apply with such force in the towns, which have often drawn their population from a wide area. This applies to London above all, whose inhabitants originate from all parts of the United Kingdom.

It may be, of course, that the original emigrant took his wife with him and that they were married before they left England. In this event, and even if the wedding took place before 1837, the date and parish of the marriage may often be found by reference to Boyd's Marriage Index, belonging to the Society of Genealogists, which I mentioned in Chapter 7.

Also in the possession of the society are many other indexes and lists and any of them may supply the vital link with an English place and family. Among them are the registers of voters or householders, indexes of apprenticeships, trade directories and marriage licences. If the earliest known ancestor were a doctor or a clergyman, then he would certainly be listed in one of the many contemporary registers held by the society. If he had attended either of the two major universities then his birthplace and parentage are likewise available.

Those with wealthy ancestors fare better than others, of course, and a rich family must have left wills, as described in Chapter 10.

Finally, for the man who has a coat-of-arms, or considers that he has a legitimate title to one, then the College of Arms will either possess his complete pedigree or else swiftly demolish his most cherished beliefs!

There is a story, no doubt apocryphal, of the upstart snob who paid a professional genealogist £50 to have his ancestry traced—and then £100 to have the results kept quiet!

18
Conclusion

Genealogy is an ideal occupation for the amateur researcher, for it is a subject which is uniquely applicable to the person concerned and which, nearly always, has been explored by no one else. One can, of course, pay a professional to do all the work but, besides being extremely expensive, this is to deprive oneself of at least half the pleasure. Watching a game may be enjoyable, but participation is to be preferred.

It may be objected that research is still not a cheap hobby, with the cost of certificates, fees, photostats and the like; but this is to exaggerate unfairly. I myself have spent a good deal of money on genealogy, but the cost has been spread over four years and probably averages less than 25p a week. In any event, there is no need to take an extreme course. One could trace only one's father's family, for instance, and pursue the research as and when the money is available.

A certain amount of professional help is a necessity, however. When one lives outside London, it is much cheaper to pay a searcher than to travel in oneself; for example, if you wish to find what the 1851 census has to say about your great-grandfather, and you know where he lived, then a professional archivist would probably find the relevant entry and send you a typewritten copy or photostat for about £1. As I explained in Chapter 4, charges are made according to the time spent, and if you are in doubt you may specify beforehand the most you wish to pay. Officials of the Public Record Office will not themselves undertake research, but they will provide the names of reputable searchers, as will most county record offices. Somerset House, unlike the Public Record Office, deals extensively with postal inquiries and they will send details of their charges to anyone who is interested. The Society of Genealogists will undertake research for moderate fees and I personally have always found them most helpful (see Appendix 1).

When seeking information from parish registers, it is best to do this yourself if at all possible. If you cannot visit the church for any reason, the vicar or clergyman will usually help, but he is entitled to receive search fees which are laid down by the Church Commissioners. Many clergymen are willing to adjust these according to the time taken or the difficulties entailed. Others again are fortunate in having members of their congregation who are themselves interested and any queries are usually passed on to them.

Finally, remember the following:

1. When writing to clergymen or to other people not professionally concerned with research, always enclose a stamped addressed envelope for their reply.

2. When copying entries from parish registers or elsewhere, write down all the details, no matter how irrelevant some may seem at the time. The name of a marriage witness, for example, may provide a crucial clue later on.

3. Never rely on memory, which can play strange tricks. Take rough notes immediately and make a fair copy as soon as possible.

4. Until it is proved wrong, accept any family story which is either discreditable or neutral; in these cases tradition is usually correct.

5. Disbelieve all family traditions which concern kinship with the noble or the wealthy. Similarity of surnames is no guarantee of relationship, and while such stories may be true, they usually are not.

6. Do not expect ages given on certificates or registers to be always accurate. Even when there is no deliberate attempt to deceive, mistakes are common.

7. Before visiting any county record office or reference library, particularly where a long journey is involved, always check beforehand that it will be open when you arrive. Particularly, never call at a church without an appointment and expect to examine the registers on demand.

8. Most record offices and reference libraries have photo-copying apparatus these days. A photostat copy is cheap and can save much labour. Above all, it does not make mistakes!

9. Never believe advertisements which promise to supply a replica of 'your' coat-of-arms for a couple of pounds. Except in a few fortuitous cases, of which the firm will be ignorant, this will belong not to your family but to another of the same name.

10. It is sometimes possible to find information by advertising in a local paper. Ask for anyone of the appropriate name who is interested in genealogy to contact you and you may find a distant relative whose research will complement your own. When I tried this for the Abbotts, I found one crank, two fortune hunters and only one genuine inquiry. Others have been more fortunate!

11. If you want a specific item of information, even if it concerns happenings of a hundred years or so ago, try asking elderly relatives before engaging in prolonged research. After I had finally worked out that the Ridleys came from Sheepy Magna, I met a second cousin of my father, who remarked casually, 'Of course they lived in Sheepy; I've seen the grave-stones there. Why didn't you ask me first?'

Why not indeed!

12. Never give up hope; if one source does not provide the information you need, try another. Remember that persever-ance is the hallmark of the true genealogist. Good hunting!

Main genealogical sources

1 *Oral tradition and family possessions*	Old letters, newspaper cuttings, diaries, Bibles, etc.
2 *Somerset House* (General Register Office, London)	(a) *Birth certificates:* Date, place, father's name and occupation, mother's maiden name (b) *Marriage certificates:* Date, place, ages, occupations, literacy, both fathers' names and occupations (c) *Death certificates:* Date, place, age, occupation, cause of death
3 *Public Record Office* (Chancery Lane, London, W.C.2)	(a) *Census returns 1841:* Names, place, ages to nearest five years, occupations, whether born in that county or not (b) *Census returns, 1851:* Names, place, ages, occupations, relationships, places of birth (c) *Census returns, 1861:* Ditto
4 *Churches*	*Registers* (a) *Baptisms:* Date, name of one or both parents, date of birth? father's occupation? (b) *Marriages:* Date, occupations? literacy? parishes of both partners? licence or banns (c) *Burials:* Date, age? occupation? relationships? (d) *Monumental inscriptions:* Dates, age? relationships?
5 *Local record offices*	(a) *Bishop's Transcripts:* As parish registers (b) *Trade directories:* Dates, occupations, addresses (c) *Wills:* Dates, occupations, wife, children, estate, etc.

5 *Local record offices* (contd.)	(d) *Marriage licences:* Dates, places, names, occupations, parents? (e) *Miscellaneous:* Printed registers, diaries, lists of voters, printed pedigrees, local histories, church-warden's accounts, etc.
6 *Reference libraries*	Printed sources (*Burke's Landed Gentry*, etc.), county histories, genealogical indexes, etc.
7 *Society of Genealogists* (37, Harrington Gardens, London, S.W.7)	Indexes, all printed sources, directories, copies of many parish registers, copies of pedigrees, many cheap and useful books and pamphlets for sale, research undertaken at reasonable cost, membership open
8 *College of Arms* (Queen Victoria Street, London, E.C.4)	All records of Herald's Visitations (seventeenth century and earlier), pedigrees of armigerous families only, research undertaken but very expensive, records not available to the general public

Appendix 2

Most common surnames

The most common surnames in England and Wales, in order of frequency, are:

1	Smith	26	Harris
2	Jones	27	Clark
3	Williams	28	Cooper
4	Taylor	29	Harrison
5	Davies	30	Ward
6	Brown	31	Martin
7	Thomas	32	Davis
8	Evans	33	Baker
9	Roberts	34	Morris
10	Johnson	35	James
11	Wilson	36	King
12	Robinson	37	Morgan
13	Wright	38	Allen
14	Wood	39	Moore
15	Thompson	40	Parker
16	Hall	41	Clarke
17	Green	42	Cook
18	Walker	43	Price
19	Hughes	44	Phillips
20	Edwards	45	Shaw
21	Lewis	46	Bennett
22	White	47	Lee
23	Turner	48	Watson
24	Jackson	49	Griffiths
25	Hill	50	Carter

This list was compiled in 1853. No national figures have been obtained since, but the overall picture is unlikely to have changed.

Appendix 3

Civil registration in the Commonwealth

Civil registration of births, marriages and deaths in the major countries of the British Commonwealth and South Africa (an asterisk indicates that some earlier records are also available):

COUNTRY	DATE OF FIRST COMPULSORY REGISTRATION	ADDRESS TO WHICH INQUIRIES SHOULD BE MADE
Australia		
New South Wales	1856	General Registry, Sydney*
Queensland	1856	Registrar-General, Brisbane*
South Australia	1842	Principal Registrar, Adelaide
Tasmania	1838	Registrar-General, Hobart*
Victoria	1853	Government Statist, Melbourne*
Western Australia	1841	Registrar-General, Perth*
Northern Territory	1874	Registrar-General, Alice Springs*
Canada		
Alberta	1885	Deputy Registrar-General, Bureau of Vital Statistics, Edmonton
British Columbia	1872	Director of Vital Statistics, Parliament Buildings, Victoria*
Manitoba	1882	Division of Vital Statistics, Department of Health and Public Welfare, 327 Legislative Building, Winnipeg*
New Brunswick	1920	Registrar-General of Vital Statistics, Department of Health, Fredericton
Newfoundland	1891	Registrar-General, Department of Health and Welfare, St John's
Nova Scotia	—	Registrar-General, Nova Scotia
Ontario	1869	Registrar-General, Ontario

Prince Edward Island	1906	Vital Statistics Branch, Department of Health and Welfare, Charlottetown
Saskatchewan	1879	Division of Vital Statistics, Department of Public Health, Regina
Yukon Territory	1898	Registrar of Vital Statistics, Administration Buildings, Dawson
Northwest Territories	1870	Registrar-General of Vital Statistics, Bureau of Northwest Territories and Yukon Affairs, Ottawa

(*Note:* Quebec has church records dating in some cases from as early as 1617. Duplicates are deposited with the Prothonotary of the Superior Court of the relevant district)

| *New Zealand* | 1848 | Registrar-General, Wellington* |

South Africa

Cape Province	1895 (births and deaths)		1812 (marriages)	
Orange Free State	1902	,,	,,	1872	,,
Transvaal	1901	,,	,,	1869	,,
Natal	1868	,,	,,	1880	,,

(Application should be made to Registrar of Births, Deaths and Marriages, c/o Population Registrar Building, Corner of Schoeman and Van der Walt Street, Pretoria, Transvaal)

Appendix 4

Pedigrees of: Abbott,
Wood,
Bull and Allday,
Ridley,
Vincent,
Drayton

b. = born
c. = very approximate
d. = died
d.y. = died young
n.i. = no issue
↓ = the line of descent continues

Single dates indicate when those so designated are known to have been alive. Most early dates are only approximate. Some dates are accurate only to two years, i.e. a burial of 1850 giving the age at death as thirty is taken to indicate the date of birth as 1820, in the absence of other evidence. It could, of course, be 1819 or even another year either way.

ABBOTT

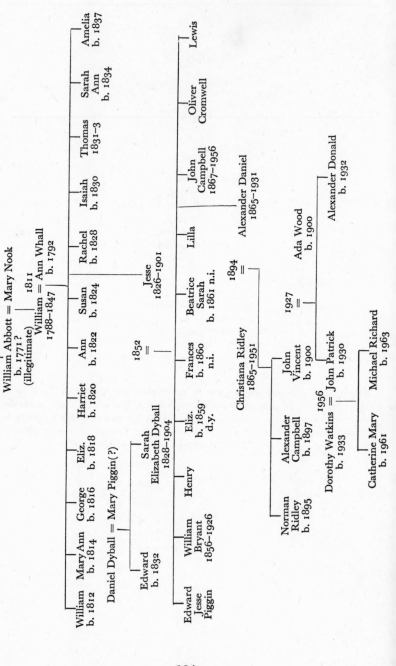

WOOD

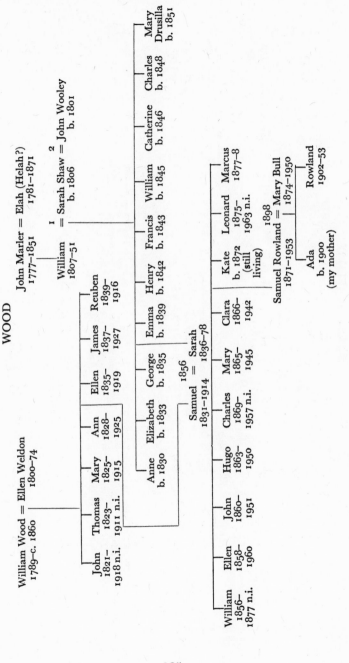

BULL and ALLDAY

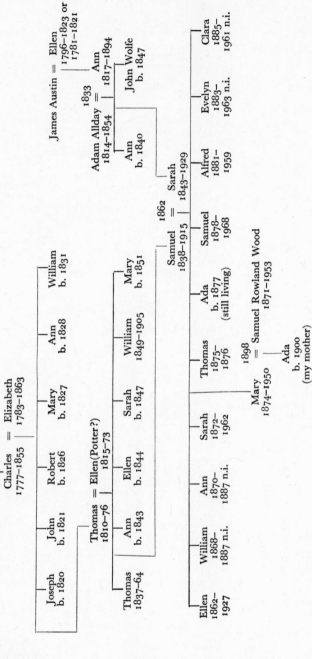

RIDLEY

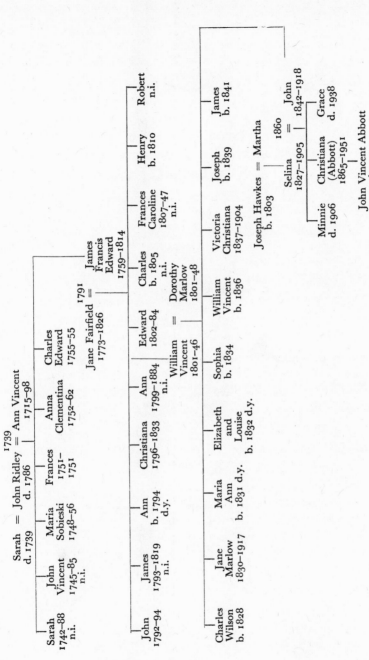

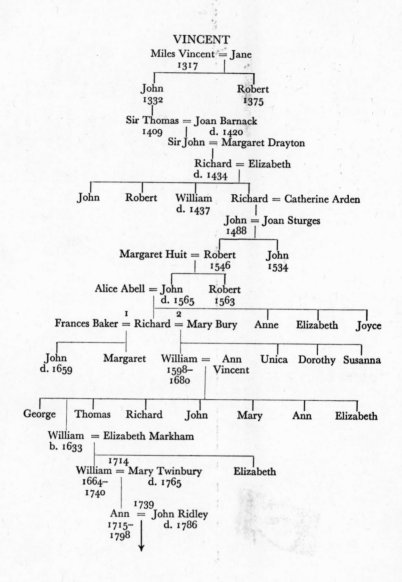

VINCENT

DRAYTON

Aubrey de Vere
1066

Aubrey de Vere = Adeliza de Clare
d. 1141

Aubrey de Vere
(Earl of Oxford)

Sir Robert = Matilda de Furnell

Sir Henry = Hildeburga
d. 1193

Sir Walter = Lucia Basset
(de Drayton)
d. 1210

Sir Henry = Ivetta de Bourdon
d. 1249

Sir Baldwin = Idonea de Gimeges
d. 1277

Sir John = Philippa de Arderne
1254–1291

Sir Henry Greene = Catherine

Sir Simon = Margaret de Lindsey
1282–1357

Sir John = Christian de Lindsey

Sir Baldwin = Alice de Prayers
(of Cranford)
d. 1395

John
d. 1424

Margaret = Sir John Vincent